DREAMS, DEEDS, AND DESTINY

Purpose and Possibility in the Space Age

By
Gwendolyn Rose Forrest

To Thomascine Ford
GRForrest '16

Strategic Book Publishing and Rights Co.

DEDICATION

*I dedicate this book to my mother, Claudia Forrest,
to my father, James Forrest, and to you,*

DREAM CATCHER

According to legend, good dreams pass through,
The hole in the dream catcher's center to,
The dreamer, while bad dreams are kept outside,
Where, at the dawning of daylight, they died.

In legend dreams drifted around, on air;
Inside of your head, they drift around there,
Until they die away, or become set,
Transformed into dreams, you cannot forget.

And dreams of destiny are the latter,
That in your life will momently matter;
To manifest the dreams of destiny,
Dream catcher, and deed doer, you must be.

CONTENTS

For your convenience in accessing ideas, the entries in this book are simultaneously presented in alphabetical and chronological order. The placement of commas gives each entry a distinct rhythm when it is read or spoken.

CHAPTERS

INTRODUCTION

In these turbulent times of economic instability, social inse-curity, and personal vulnerability, there is a need for a world-view that provides us with purpose and possibility. *Dreams, Deeds, and Destiny* does this. Starting as commentary on the human experience, this book evolved into a day-by-day guide for achieving success and happiness in the space age. Erudite and engaging, its goal is to help you create a purposeful human experience every day. More than a collection of secular affir-mations, meditations, and observations, in its entirety, *Dreams, Deeds, and Destiny* is

A PHILOSOPHY OF HOPE

We went to the mountaintop, nothing was there,
Save snow, ice, and wind, in the rarified air;
No god, or goddess, or other deity,
We found on the mountaintop, or in the sea.

So we traded temples, for a telescope,
Giving us vision, of a much greater scope;
No longer limited, to the blue planet,
From out in the cosmos, we look upon it.

Had we not dreamed, and done deeds, we did somehow,
We would not be living, in the space age, now.
With space ships, space probes, and a space station,
We are expanding our space exploration.

As the cosmos is tilted toward success,
We tilt this way, and dreams tend to manifest;
So do not devalue your dreams or self-worth,
For you have purposes, to fulfill on earth.

When you adopt this Philosophy of Hope,
With life challenges, you'll creatively cope;
Now tune into your intuition, and see,
Your dreams and deeds co-create your destiny.

JANUARY

JANUARY 1

ABOUT COSMIC POWER

They whirl on myriad courses through space,
    Empowered by cosmic power, not chance;
Continuously, they evolve in place,
    And interdependently dance a dance.

While beyond, the Milky Way Galaxy,
    Beyond, the telescopes and space probes' sights,
Far beyond, our farthest-fetched fantasy,
    Billions of bodies dance in far-flung flights.

Infinite bodies whirling in orbit,
    Dance in a cosmos that is marvelous;
All unequivocally exhibit,
    That comic power is ubiquitous.

We whirl on myriad courses through space,
    Empowered by cosmic power, not chance;
Continuously, we evolve in place,
    And interdependently dance a dance.

Irrespective of affiliation,
    Religion, gender, IQ, creed, color,
Or any other classification,
    Not one of us is above, another.

Yet cosmic power, in us, and our deeds,
    Is not identically, reflected;
Individualization intercedes,
    And power's personally, projected.

Gwendolyn Rose Forrest

Now that you know about cosmic power,
    Empowering what was, is, and will be,
Can you accept that you have this power,
    And that you co-create your destiny?

JANUARY 2

ABOUT PRAYER

Recall some of the prayers you prayed,
Last month, last year, or last decade;
Now think how life would be, today,
Had they manifested, that way.

Some of the prayers you prayed, back then,
Were compromises, you made when,
You doubted you could carry through,
On the deeds that were yours, to do.

Other prayers prayed, so fervently,
Were expressions of, expediency;
Begging, bargaining for relief,
They promised things, beyond belief.

As in the cosmos, needs are known,
Before to you a need is shown,
You need not bargain, or beseech,
About needs known, before, you speak.

So instead of supplication,
Make your prayer, an affirmation,
And expect success, when you do,
Affirm whatever, you want to.

JANUARY 3

ABUNDANCE

Relax and trust in the cosmos to work;
This does not mean that your duties, you shirk,
By acting in an unwise wanton way,
Wasting tomorrow's resources, today.

But anticipate abundance! Don't doubt,
The cosmos will bring abundance, about;
Anticipate abundance does abound,
And you will find abundance, all around.

JANUARY 4

ABUSES

Undulating waves splash upon the shore,
Exposing abuses that heretofore,
Were hidden by plastic, concrete, and steel,
Abuses we know, pollute, maim, and kill.

We blast off mountaintops, sully the seas,
And plant landmines, instead of planting trees;
Repeated abuses will by, and by,
Turn flowing rivers and aquifers, dry.

People wield power, but we abuse it;
Earth is our homeland, and we misuse it.
Abuses, of the past and present must,
Arise in the future, and abuse us.

So let us not, for another moment,
Abuse the earth, and its environment;
Promoting our planet's conservation,
This is the business of every nation.

JANUARY 5

AFFIRMATIONS

Affirmations are positive,
    And positive, in every way;
So never put a negative,
    In those you conceive, write, or say.

And affirmations that digress,
    Are not futile, for they don't rest,
Until they've helped to manifest,
    Not just good, but better, what's *best!*

JANUARY 6

AFFIRMATIONS AND EXPECTATIONS

Affirm what you want, for your life, each day;
Then expect what you want, to come, your way.
An affirmation is what, you conceive;
An expectation is what, you believe.

So beforehand, act as if you've received,
Whatever it is, your mind has conceived;
For want and fulfillment to coincide,
Affirmations and expectations jibe.

JANUARY 7

AIR

You could not see the seagull soar,
    If unseen air was not stirring,
Nor could you hear the lion's roar,
    If air was not, maneuvering.

It's air against wings wide, in flight,
    Enabling the seagull, to soar,
And air on vocal cords, so slight,
    That enables the lion's roar.

The air of thought, creates the scene,
    That is for us, reality,
And makes things seen, and things, unseen,
    A fact for us, not fantasy.

Since what life is, and what life's naught,
    From our first breath, till our last one,
Depends upon, the air of thought,
    Think of ways, to make your life fun.

JANUARY 8

APPEARANCES

Like the bulk of the iceberg is not seen,
　　Because it lies below the ocean's plane,
The effects of your efforts are not seen,
　　Until life unfolds, its following frame.

So if you are doing the best, you can,
　　But your best does not appear, good enough,
Do not be deceived; instead take a stand,
　　Against appearances, and call their bluff.

Refuse to give up your best, right away,
　　For appearances are not all, they seem;
And appearances could this very day,
　　Be changed by your best, to a fulfilled dream.

JANUARY 9

ATTITUDE

Attitude gives you latitude,
 To fly high, or stay, on the ground,
And attitude adds magnitude,
 To choosing not to stay, earth bound.

Attitude decides altitude;
 This means the height, to which you'll fly;
So summon up, your fortitude,
 To keep your attitude, sky high!

JANUARY 10

AUGUST THINGS

White smoke curls from chimneys, with flair,
Floats, then fades into frigid air,
Surrounding, the snow-capped rooftops,
Contrasting with busy bus stops,
And bustling city streets, below,
Soiled by, melting ice, slush, and snow.

In cities, snowcapped, rooftops share,
With mountaintops, snowcapped, and fair,
A poignant, pristine majesty,
And boldly breathtaking beauty,
That awes, because from whence, it springs;
Snowcapped rooftops are august things!

JANUARY 11

BALLOT OR BULLET

Too often, in many societies,
Where there exists glaring inequities,
Segments considered, unworthy of note,
Are defrauded of, or denied, the vote.

Whenever segments are disenfranchised,
They smolder, and ultimately, up rise;
However, before an up rise is set,
There is a choice, the ballot or bullet.

The ballot's prone to, manipulation,
And the bullet to, annihilation;
So in the long run, this is the best bet:
It's the ballot, in lieu of, the bullet.

JANUARY 12

BARE BOUGHS

Bare boughs beneath a steel gray sky,
They're not inactive arms held high;
Though they show no sign, outwardly,
Of internal, activity,
Bare boughs house, absolute knowing,
That budding boughs, shall be showing.

Like bare boughs house, internally,
Invisible activity,
You must house in your heart, and mind,
When you can see, no outward sign,
An active, absolute knowing,
That fulfilled dreams, shall be showing.

JANUARY 13

BE

Sometimes you should not say, nor do, but BE,
BE as mute and motionless, as a tree,
BE in a peaceful frame of mind, freely,
Communing with the cosmos, completely!

JANUARY 14

BE AUTHENTIC

Don't think you are damned in the world,
　　Of no worth, and unfit for joy,
If you are a girl, loving a girl,
　　Or a boy, who's loving, a boy.

When others dictate, how you live,
　　You're a rudderless roustabout;
Adrift in vague alternatives,
　　Unauthentic, you live in doubt.

Be authentic. Validate you,
　　For if you've not known this, thus far,
The universe empowers you;
　　This makes you of worth, as you are.

JANUARY 15

BEAT THE BLAHS

A lone plane drones through a slate-colored sky;
On salt-stained streets, soiled vehicles drive by,
Tall stacks of snow and slush that slowing melt.
Behind gray clouds, the sun is barely felt.

In a bitter breeze, bare boughs slowly sway,
Resembling bare bones, seen in an x-ray;
Even evergreens seem to don, dull gray,
On dark dreary days, determined to stay.

And often on dark dreary days, like these,
The blahs descend, besieging us, with ease;
So beat the blahs, while enthusing yourself.
Do a deed of kindness, for someone else.

JANUARY 16

BECOMING

As you're evolving each day, in some way,
You are becoming, in some way, each day.

And every, becoming is different;
Therefore no becoming is redundant.

So as you're evolving, through the unknown,
Know you are becoming, into your own.

JANUARY 17

BEEN THERE, DONE THAT

Have you been there? Have you done that?
    If so, you've new scenes, to explore.
Have you been there? Have you done that?
    If so, you've higher heights, to soar.

If you've been there, or you've done that,
    Then for you, there and that, are gone;
You cannot go back, redo that.
    Life either drives, or drags, you on.

JANUARY 18

BELIEF

When looking at the little humming bird,
That it can fly at all appears absurd;
At fifty strokes per second, its wings speed,
But look like they lack power, to succeed.

Nevertheless, the little humming bird,
Spurning the skepticism, it has heard,
Believes its wings possess enough power,
And it does fly from flower, to flower.

Belief packs power, and belief, we find,
Is not in a ritual, rite, or rhyme,
And not in a symbol, nor in a sign;
Belief dwells in the mystery, of mind.

And belief helps change concepts, we conceive,
From concepts into concretes, we receive;
Life is livable, or unlivable,
Because, belief is so *formidable!*

JANUARY 19

THE BELL

(Remembering Jeanne, my friend)

Beneath the bell, three belles believed they'd be,
    Permanently,
But life proved this belief a fallacy;
    Predictably!

So when the bell tolls, it tells,
    Us life is a mystery;
And when the bell tolls, its tales,
    It tells us of destiny.

JANUARY 20

BEND

You have to be flexible,
In order to be able,
To cope with the stress, and strife,
Stirred up by, the storms of life.

So it is better, to bend,
Like a willow, in the wind,
And some alterations make,
Rather than not bend, but break.

JANUARY 21

BEST FRIEND

The little girl said, "My friend, to the end;
You always will be, my very best friend."
Then, so she could see her best friend clearer,
The little girl deftly, wiped the mirror.

If you don't know, unlike this little girl,
Who, should be your best friend, in all the world,
Look, in the mirror, because, no one else,
Should, be better than you are, to yourself.

JANUARY 22

BIRTHDAYS

Because today was Bert's birthday,
　　Beth sang, "Happy birthday to you!"
He thanked her, and went on, to say,
　　"Of birthdays, I have had a few."

She asked, "Do you plan to retire?
　　He replied, "I'm still having fun,
And it is not my heart's desire,
　　To, retire, at age ninety-one."

"Birthdays should not bamboozle us,
　　Or be our determining gauge.
Birthdays don't dictate, what we must;
　　They count chronological age."

JANUARY 23

BITTERSWEET

Wandering on the wind-swept beach,
 With the snow clinging to his shoes,
Will wondered if, distance would breach,
 Their love, and Lil's love, he would lose.

To love makes us, vulnerable,
 To the cold, along with the heat,
For love, unlike, in a fable,
 It's ever after, bittersweet.

JANUARY 24

BLANKETS

Spontaneously, without sound,
Swirling snowflakes slowly drift down;
For miles, and miles, and miles around,
They spread a blanket, on the ground.

And like snowflakes blanket, the ground,
Spontaneously, without sound,
When sometimes peace seems, not around,
It blankets us in peace, profound.

Gwendolyn Rose Forrest

JANUARY 25

THE BLUES

It is a fact, when,
    You stay, with the blues,
Too frequently, then,
    You pay, heavy dues,
        For housing, the blues,
            Behind, your mind's door,
        To discolor, views,
            Right down, to their core.

Therefore, when the blues,
    Tries to stay, around,
Steadfastly refuse,
    To remain, so down;
        Let thoughts, you peruse,
            Cause your mind, to soar,
        And this makes the blues,
            Stay with you, no more!

JANUARY 26

BORN TO BE FREE

Fettering the freedom of another,
Binds both of the parties to each other;
So neither is free, to fly high, in flight.
Both are bound down, by the fettered one's plight.

So whether lover, relative, or foe,
Fettering freedom brings both parties woe;
To pursue a personal destiny,
Every person born is born to be free.

JANUARY 27

BOUNCE BACK

To play on this basketball court, called life,
You are going to have some stress, and strife;
Life does not promise, you won't be knocked down,
But it does promise that you can, rebound.

When you undertake an uphill-work time,
You cannot have someone else, make your climb;
And when you're knocked down, every now and then,
You have to bounce back, again, and again.

If you are feeling fraught, fearful, or frail,
As though your attempts are to no, avail,
Set you sight beyond, appearances' veil,
And persevere, if you want to prevail.

So when life seems to hold success, at bay,
And perseverance starts to slip, away,
Persevere some more, and you'll find, in fact,
That you have bounced back, and bounced back, intact.

JANUARY 28

BOXED-IN

Too frequently, we live boxed-in,
    A box not made of steel, or stone;
Instead the box, we are locked in,
    Is the boxed-in mind that, we own.

Disavowing, anomalies,
    And kowtowing to, phantom fear,
While worshipping, orthodoxies,
    To absurdities, we adhere.

So we avoid terrain, unknown,
    And even after, we've been shown,
That known terrain, has been outgrown,
    We stay there, for the known *is known!*

However, to live not boxed-in,
    We must show the courage, to tread,
Unknown terrain, although frightened,
    Or exist boxed-in, like the dead.

JANUARY 29

THE BRISK BREEZE

A gaggle of geese, on the lake,
  Out where the water does not freeze,
Do not make the waves, in their wake;
  The waves are made by the brisk breeze.

And the brisk breeze, buffets a boat,
  From which three men fish, doggedly;
Each man wears a cap, and a coat,
  For the brisk breeze blows, intensely.

Showing no bias, the brisk breeze,
  Buffeting both the boat, and men,
Buffets dry leaves, clinging to trees,
  And this renders most trees, barren.

And the brisk breeze, buffeting all,
  Evokes this realization:
In winter, spring, summer, and fall,
  Connected is every person.

JANUARY 30

BY THE BORDER

We live by the border between,
Life and death, from cradle, to grave;
Perched precariously are seen,
Parent - child, saint - knave, master - slave.

And life by the border breeds fear,
In some severe, in others, mild,
Knowing that death is waiting near -,
By the border, all of the while.

Though by the border, death does wait,
Speaking metaphorically,
Do not let death usurp life's state,
Until, it does literally.

JANUARY 31

BYWAYS

Deaf and despondent, in a deep dark daze,
Some drag through life, like a snail in a maze,
While breathless and blinded, in a hot haze,
Others race through life, like a fire ablaze.

Neither drag though life, in a deep dark daze,
Nor race through it, in a hasty, hot haze;
Instead, enjoy exploring life's byways,
And you'll experience life, in new ways,

FEBRUARY

FEBRUARY 1

CASTINGS

(For Anita, my daughter)

Her smile is cast from the sun, at sunrise,
And twinkling stars are the casts, for her eyes.
Fetching is her infectious, laughter;
Comely is the way, the cosmos casts her.

She is a one of a kind, true treasure,
With a worldly worth having, no measure;
My kudos, to the cosmos which wrought her,
And cast her to be, my darling daughter.

Daughters, dragonflies, daisies, and the sun,
Come into existence, for a reason;
In the cosmic play, all are cast to play,
The part only he, she, or it, can play.

FEBRUARY 2

CELEBRATE

(For Johnnie, my twin cousin)

Whether by yourself,
Or with someone else,
Don't abide delay;
Do it right away.

And do it, with zest;
Never be modest.
Let your joy run rife;
Celebrate your life!

FEBRUARY 3

CENTER OF CALM

I have a center of calm, deep within,
That's calm as the center, of the whirlwind;
When all around me, worries are whirling,
Screeching and screaming, swirling and twirling,
My center of calm, made of cosmic power,
It keeps me calm, every hour upon hour.

Within my center of calm, there I steep,
Centered in cosmic power, where I keep,
Undaunted by uncertainty, and doubt,
Unworried by worries whirling, about;
As calm as the center, of the whirlwind,
I remain calm from day's start through night's end.

FEBRUARY 4

CERTAIN UNCERTAINTY

Life is full of certain uncertainty,
For it is an unfolding mystery;
Whenever we feel, we've figured life out,
It certainly does rekindle our doubt.

When we die, uncertainty goes away;
Alive, we must live with it, day by day.
We do not control all of life's aspects;
Our control's over efforts, not effects.

Yet curbs on our control, too often go,
Understated, while control's stated so,
That we assume responsibility,
For effects, we do not decide, wholly.

Control over efforts, and not effects,
Makes life uncertain, in certain respects,
But lacking in certain uncertainty,
Lackluster and limited, life would be.

FEBRUARY 5

CHANGE

To change imperceptibly,
    It only takes an instant,
And as things change constantly,
    Change is the common constant.

If everything stays the same,
    In exactly the same ways,
An unfulfilled, longed-for aim,
    It stays out of range, always.

The present becomes passé;
    To the nouveau, it gives way.
Then the nouveau has its sway,
    Before, it passes away.

So we are born, pliable,
    Because all things rearrange,
And if we stay flexible,
    We capably cope, with change.

FEBRUARY 6

CHANGING SEASONS

The winter, spring, summer, and fall,
They're changing seasons, one and all;
One season wanes, another dawns,
With constantly changing, seasons.

So with gusto, let us embrace,
Each season we have left, to face;
One season wanes, another dawns,
And we're changed, by changing seasons.

FEBRUARY 7

CHARITY

To be charitable responsibly,
Requires much more than, generosity;
Certain circumstances, we cannot change,
For certain things aren't ours to, rearrange.

Enabling another's dependency,
Makes no contribution to charity;
In some circumstances, though this seems cold,
It is more charitable to withhold.

FEBRUARY 8

CHILDREN CREATING CHILDREN

Children creating children,
    Requires little or no skill;
Children who create children,
    Too often tread life's treadmill.

As a child, Mae's grandmother had children;
Later, Mae's mother continued, this trend.
At age fourteen, Mae became a mother,
But she treated her son, like a brother.

Children creating children,
    It is such a short-lived, thrill;
Children, who create children,
    Too often tread life's treadmill.

To flee a life of poverty, and pain,
Like his father, Mae's son, rode the fast lane;
One cold night Mae's son was shot, in the head;
Seven days later, he was declared dead.

Children creating children,
    Creates an ominous chill;
Children, who create children,
    Too often tread life's treadmill.

Mae was barely fourteen, when she birthed him;
He was barely fourteen, when she earthed him.
Too soon, too many children are dying;
Too soon, too many loved ones left crying.

Children creating children,
    Makes a societal ill;
So let us teach all children,
    To, circumvent life's treadmill.

FEBRUARY 9

CHOICES

About your choices, and opportunity,
Other people's voices give advice, freely.

When choices in your mine, diverge far and wide,
Where do you find, a dependable guide?

In you is a guide, in which you can confide;
Then you must decide, if by it, you'll abide.

FEBRUARY 10

CIRCUMSTANCES

Some people live in poverty, from birth,
Until they exhale their last breath, on earth;
So if you have sufficient food, to eat,
Clean clothes, to wear, a decent place, to sleep,
Self-expression outlets, and good health too,
Count yourself, among the fortunate few.

However, if among the few, you're not,
Be grateful anyway, for what, you've got.
As a rule be grateful, rather than curse,
For your circumstances could be much worse.

FEBRUARY 11

CITY SONG

The city sings, a complex song,
A song it sings, day and night long,
A song composed of steel, and stone,
And things that sing songs, of their own.

On city sidewalks, quartets sing,
And boom boxes cause ears, to ring,
While tongues familiar, and tongues strange,
Sing till they fade, from hearing range.

Upon the elevated tracks,
The el trains sing their clicks and clacks,
While sirens sing, throughout the night,
As do revelers making light.

The city's song is distinct from,
The song the countryside does hum;
Except, in quasi-quiet dark,
They sound the same, inside a park.

The city sings, a complex song,
In which diverse groups sing, along,
In harmony, for the most part;
The city is a work of art.

FEBRUARY 12

CLAMOROUS COMPANY

Some of us keep clamorous company,
With radio, stereo, or TV;
We prattle on, in idle chitchat, too.
Any, clamorous company, will do!

Our innermost thoughts, we're afraid to hear,
And clamorous company cloaks, our fear;
With no clamorous company around,
A clearer knowledge of self would be found.

FEBRUARY 13

CLOSE PROXIMITY

About our days, we are blasé,
When death is make-believe child's play,
Or faraway phenomenon,
That happens to a distant one.

When death calls on one we care for,
It moves into the space, next door,
To wait, in close proximity,
Until, it calls, personally.

With death in close proximity,
The next day is no certainty;
So until, on you, death does call,
Enjoy every day, one and all.

FEBRUARY 14

CLOSE TO HOME

In a complex, global community,
Is world peace a real possibility?
Or is it a concept, with some appeal,
But one few believe, can become real?

World peace, when considered practically,
Is achievable in society;
World peace does not start, in a far-off place,
For it starts, close to home, in inner space.

FEBRUARY 15

CLOSED DOORS

Much is said about open doors,
    Offering opportunity,
But little's said about closed doors,
    And how, they work, in life's journey.

Closed doors encountered on our way,
    Aren't there to thwart, purposelessly;
Closed doors occur, so we don't stray,
    And lose sight of our destiny.

FEBRUARY 16

CLOUDS AND DREAMS

Clouds are wispy, whimsical things,
That change with our imaginings;
If we imagine, then clouds can,
Change from a mouse, into a man.

Like clouds, dreams are whimsical things,
That change with our imaginings,
But dreams persisting, in the mind,
These dreams are the destiny kind.

So start fulfilling dreams, you find,
Persisting, inside of, your mind,
And if you persist, you will see,
Your dreams become reality.

FEBRUARY 17

COCOON

Like a caterpillar, in a cocoon,
Secludes itself from everything, outside,
Seclude yourself in silence; there abide.

Secluded in silence, you'll be immune,
To everything, except life within you;
Invigorating life, it renews you.

And like a caterpillar, from cocoon,
Emerges brand new, as a butterfly,
You'll emerge renewed, and ready to fly.

FEBRUARY 18

CONSEQUENCES

Occasionally, we stumble, or fall,
For we are only human, after all,
And on occasion, we must watch and wait,
While to a mistake, a loved one heads straight.

In order to understand what life takes,
Each one has to make his/her own, mistakes;
Mistakes are merely, *consequences* earned,
While learning life lessons that must be learned.

FEBRUARY 19

CONSTANT COMPANION

Patiently waiting to make them, hard and cold,
Death is a constant companion, to the old,
And in due time, death will devour them, from sight,
Like the sun at sundown is devoured, by night.

Yet death is a constant companion, to all,
Whether it's our winter, spring, summer, or fall;
Furthermore, in the final analysis,
Death devours us all. Nobody can resist.

And like the sun at dawn, departs from the night,
When we depart from life, we depart death's sight,
But alive, out of death's sight, we cannot run;
So alive, death is our constant companion.

FEBRUARY 20

THE CORRIDOR

Between life's closed door, and open door,
Intervening is the corridor,
Wherein, we must spend some time, before,
We can proceed through life's open, door.

This time may be of long duration,
Filled with fear, and fraught with frustration,
Or it may be, on the other hand,
Extremely short, and it may be grand.

In either event, the corridor,
Between life's closed door, and open door,
Gives us time, to reassess our route,
And the aims in life, we are about.

FEBRUARY 21

COUNSEL FROM WITHIN

Do not ask, around and about,
    For advice on what, you should do,
As advice that comes from without,
    Most likely is not right, for you.

By being your own counselor,
    Other people, you will prevent,
From acting as your advisor,
    Lending advice, too loosely lent.

Thus you won't have, without a doubt,
    Others to fault, or to defend,
Advice from around, and about,
    Not counsel, coming from, within.

When other's opinions, you need,
    Your counsel gives such directions;
Then, your counsel helps you, to heed,
    What, you deem, are sound suggestions.

Your challenges would not, be yours,
    Had you not, their resolutions;
Counsel from within, really scores,
    By giving you, right solutions.

FEBRUARY 22

CRAB APPLE DREAMS

It's a miniature apple,
　　That looks a lot like, a cherry;
It's a diminutive apple,
　　That's small as a small, strawberry.

It's a Lilliputian apple,
　　That alone is barely a bite,
But the red, bite-size crab apple,
　　By the bushel's a mighty, mite.

Your dream is like a crab apple;
　　Alone, it's insignificant.
Add deeds and your dream is able,
　　To do what a dream alone can't.

FEBRUARY 23

CRITICAL THINKING

Like reading is not a clever trick,
   But skill acquired, in and out of school,
Critical thinking is not magic,
   But skill acquired, and a useful tool.

So learners, without an exception,
   Learn to cogitate, critically;
To give this task, your best reception,
   Adopt a "can do" philosophy.

And teachers, do not shirk your duty,
   By acquiescing in mimicry;
No matter what the subject may be,
   You're to teach to think, critically.

FEBRUARY 24

CROWS, CLOUDS, AND CONSEQUENCES

To the woodpecker pecking at a tree,
The crows cawed, "Follow us!" clamorously,
Causing some cumulus clouds, scudding by,
To cover the sun, and darkened the sky.

Like crows, your ego calls clamorously,
For you to follow it, exclusively,
But when you do, you cover up your sun,
And cause dark consequences, when you're done.

FEBRUARY 25

CUES

Contrasting conspicuously, with grays,
Commonly seen, on February days,
In a collage of color, rarely seen,
February flowers bloom, on the scene.

Fresh, flamboyant, February flowers,
They are cues showing us, in our gray hours,
That in the midst of uniformity,
We can bloom amid, mediocrity.

FEBRUARY 26

CURRENTS

Small ground squirrels, after peering around,
Cautiously graze in the grass, on the ground,
While vivid sailboards, kite boards, and kites share,
With seagulls, unseen, currents in the air.

Unseen currents billowing, in the breeze,
Caress the arms of those wearing, short sleeves;
While they are invisible, to the eye,
Their presence is felt, when they're passing by.

Unseen, life's gifts circulate, everywhere,
On unseen currents, like those in the air,
And from unseen currents, life's gifts do fall,
When, we are not, expecting them, at all.

Gwendolyn Rose Forrest

FEBRUARY 27

THE CURTAIN

Because the curtain does conceal,
    What lies beyond that, we can't see,
We think the curtain can't reveal,
    What is not now, but is to be.

Yet at times, we pierce the curtain,
    Made of present, reality,
And at these times, we ascertain,
    A glimpse of what is yet to be.

FEBRUARY 28

THE CYCLE OF CONTINUITY

The span to age sixty seems long, at sixteen;
At sixty, the span seems so short, in between.
The cycle of continuity is birth,
Procreation, death; then it returns to birth.

In winter, the white of a snow-covered scene,
Would have us believe, the scene never was green,
But in spring, the green in the same scenery,
It proves the cycle of continuity.

But don't confuse continuity, with same;
Creation, not duplication, is the aim;
An occurrence, whether negative, or nice,
The self-same occurrence does not occur, twice.

The cycle of continuity, ensures,
That change and diversity ever, endures;
That is, the cycle of continuity,
Also perpetuates possibility.

Gwendolyn Rose Forrest

FEBRUARY 29

CYCLICAL LEAP DAY

As cyclical leap day,
    Comes once every fourth year,
To ensure that its stay,
    Is full of cheer, while here,
Make sure that every day,
    Of each and every year,
In each and every way,
    Is just chocked full of cheer!

MARCH

MARCH 1

DANCE! DANCE! DANCE!

(For Andrea, my granddaughter)

Dancing to rhythms that only she knows,
The brass ballerina twirls on tiptoes;
Elegantly, with head and hands held high,
This dainty dancer reaches for the sky.

Bassari women, hipbones in motion,
Dance in the painting, with much emotion;
Hips keeping time, with their head, hands, and feet,
These dancers too, dance to, a private beat.

Dance! Dance! Dance! Like these other dancers do;
Dance to the rhythms, heard by only you;
If you heed the rhythms, your heart does beat,
You'll dance through life, with hips, head, hands, and feet.

Gwendolyn Rose Forrest

MARCH 2

DANDELIONS

Think of die-hard dandelions, today,
And how they blossom, wherever, they may.
These pretty little blossoms, yellow and bright,
Turn into pretty little seeds, of white,
Which are blown away upon, a brisk breeze,
To blossom later, wherever, they please.

Die-hard dandelions, from roots, to seeds,
Are resilient plants, we have labeled, weeds,
But their resilience, we should imitate;
Cut down they rebound, and proliferate.
Cut down by cares, we don't have to stay down,
But like die-hard dandelions, rebound!

MARCH 3

DARE TO DREAM

Dare to dream, and you make your life flower.
Dare not to dream, and diffuse your power.
Where you are now, and where you want to go,
Are derived from the dreams, you dare, to sow.

So when you dream, dare to dream, daringly,
And do not dream, daring dreams, sparingly;
As your dreams design your reality,
Dare to dream, and design your destiny.

MARCH 4

DAWN

Making no noise, an immaculate dawn,
As innocent as a freshly foaled fawn,
Glides across the sky, with no backward glance;
Assiduously, she makes her advance.

Putting her phantom feet down, daintily,
And discharging duties, diligently,
Dawn delivers to us a dewy day,
To use or abuse as we choose, today.

MARCH 5

DAYS

(Remembering Jimmy D, my father)

In the days, before my dear daddy died,
    My days flowed along, according to plan;
My steps were sure, unbroken was my stride,
    And the sun shone brightly, over the land.

In a daze, the day, my dear daddy died,
    My whole world shifted, and I could not stand.
My day was so dark, that I cried and cried;
    Yet the sun shone brightly, over the land.

In the days, since my dear daddy's demise,
    My days flow fast, though time's hourglass, like sand;
So I try to keep tears, out of my eyes,
    And enjoy each day, as best, as I can.

The seconds we're sad, add up to days lost;
    The moments we're mad, carry the same cost.
There's no regaining days lost, or their cost;
    So of days remaining, have few days lost.

MARCH 6

DEATH WITH DIGNITY

When one is knocking hard, upon death's door,
And one's quality of life, is no more,
Laws letting one chose to die, humanely,
Make sound sense, when death is a certainty.

Thus there are times, assisted suicide,
Is an option that's clearly justified;
Prolonging flesh functions, excessively,
Is death, denying death with dignity.

MARCH 7

DECIDE

Would you like to move, a mountain,
    And subdue an insurgent sea,
Or from your dreams, forge a fountain,
    That produces prosperity?

Before you say, this can't be done,
    Decide to make your dreams come true,
For destiny denies no one,
    Doing what he or she can do.

So decide, what needs to be done;
    Then act upon what, you decide.
Every deed, you have ever done,
    You have done, because you have tried.

Decide, and galvanize power;
    Don't decide, and be paralyzed.
Decide, and in this self-same hour,
    Your dreams start to be realized.

MARCH 8

DECLARATION

When I let others sail my ship, to shore,
The weeping willow wept for me, galore;
O weeping willow, weep for me, no more.

I'm set from bow, to stern, from aft, to fore,
To sail on seas, I've chosen to explore;
O weeping willow, weep for me, no more.

On seas of self-discovery, I'll soar,
Reaching heights, unreachable, heretofore;
O weeping willow, weep for me, no more.

This declaration will forevermore,
Inside of my mind, remain at its fore;
O weeping willow, weep for me, NO MORE!

MARCH 9

DEEP

The deep is not only, under the sea,
And known for inaccessibility;
As a state of mind, accessed, anywhere,
The deep is in existence, everywhere.

So dive into the deep that's, unbroken;
Commune what you will, with words, unspoken,
And shortly, from the deep, you will have heard,
Profundities revealed, without a word.

MARCH 10

DEMONSTRATION AND ALLUSION

Beneath blue sky float fluffy clouds of white,
Above light green leaves, basking in sunlight,
Atop tall trees that formerly were bare,
Now, exhibiting, a full head of hair.

Sparkling like diamonds, soft ice on the lake,
Melts day by day, as the lake comes awake,
While mesas, marshes, and meadows begin,
To bloom, like grassland and woodlands, again.

Sweet scents of crocuses, and daffodils,
Waft across the formerly fallow fields,
As mating calls, of cardinals, and wrens,
Mix with the calls, of red breasted, robins.

Denizens of every ilk feel desire,
Raging hot inside of them, like wildfire;
Chipmunk chases chipmunk, dove chases dove,
Even the naked apes' thoughts turn, to love.

Sights, sounds, scents, and sexual sensation,
Escalate, in a grand celebration,
Of life regenerating everything;
Regeneration reigns supreme, in spring.

And the spring's perennial profusion,
It's both demonstration, and allusion,
To the regeneration, we know when,
We too are renewed, every now and then.

MARCH 11

DESIGNED DYNAMIC

Eat, and be eaten, till atop the food chain,
Where minute microbes start the process again;
While it may appear that death is running rife,
This is the process, perpetuating life.

Moment by moment, and minute by minute,
All things are in motion, changing bit by bit;
For twenty-four seven, three-six-five, or six,
Life is definitely designed, dynamic!

MARCH 12

DIFFERENCES

When observed from one point of view,
    People the whole wide world around,
Display their differences through,
    Different tastes, scents, sights, and sounds.

But from another, point of view,
    Differences, cleverly say,
We are similarities, too,

D I A D W
I N   I A
S   F Y
P   F
L   E
A   R
Y   E
E   N
D   T

MARCH 13

DISCOURSE AND DEEDS

Vonnny visits the pond, each afternoon,
With a tin in hand and the air is soon,
Alive with a flurry of flapping wings,
As flocks of hungry fowls seek what, he brings.

Several birds come out of the water,
And to Vonny, they clumsily saunter;
Looking amusingly awkward, on land,
Some of the bolder birds eat from, his hand!

When Vonny says, "I'll return tomorrow,"
None of his feathered friends, display sorrow,
For seagulls and sparrows, geese and ducks, too,
Know his words are his bond, to follow through.

To do deeds you say you will do, as planned,
Can you be counted upon, like this man?
In discourse you say, whatever you may,
While deeds demonstrate, you mean what you say.

MARCH 14

DO GOOD

Because bad things can and do,
Befall good people, like you,
It's not a good reason to,
Behave in a bad way, too.

Both the bad, and good, you do,
Like a boomerang, you threw,
Circle and come back, to you;
So do good, whate'er, you do.

MARCH 15

DO YOUR KIDS A KINDNESS

The mind of a newborn, like a blank slate,
Is etched upon from the newborn's birth date,
With numerous norms, society formed,
A long time before, the newborn, was born.

Consequently, do your kids a kindness;
Allow them to pursue, their happiness.
Convey to them customs aren't set, in stone,
And let them create customs of, their own.

MARCH 16

DON'T FRET

Don't fret any upset,
　　You meet along your way;
If you do, upsets met,
　　Continue to replay.

Don't fret any upset,
　　Or let upsets run rife,
And you'll never regret,
　　That upsets ran your life.

Don't fret any upset,
　　Or let it drag you down;
No upset, has as yet,
　　Put you under the ground.

Don't fret any upset,
　　Into a tsunami;
Instead, get yourself set,
　　To savor victory!

MARCH 17

DOORS AND MONKEY BARS

When closing life's doors, now and then,
    Present you with a trying time,
Recall climbing monkey bars when,
    You performed your initial climb.

The first bar climbed was easy, though,
    You likely clung to the next one;
Only by stretching, could you go,
    On climbing until, you were done.

Like monkey bars, you did master,
    Life's door, currently in your clasp,
You'll close easier, and faster,
    Stretching, for the next door, you'll grasp.

MARCH 18

DOUBT

No doubt, doubt causes discomfort,
    And double doubt is doubly bad;
So we would like to cut it short,
    The doubt we wish, we never had.

Yet ditching doubt, on the double,
    Without any hesitation,
Could end up doubling, our trouble,
    While ending, our vacillation.

There's no doubt, doubt helps us discern,
    Fallacy, from that which is fact;
Then we must decide, if what's learned,
    Is enough, upon which, to act.

MARCH 19

DOWN IS DOWN AND UP IS UP

If you must tear down another,
To lift up yourself, don't bother,
For tearing down, does not lift up,
As down is down, and up is up.

So if you want to lift yourself,
Do it, by lifting someone else;
You can't tear down, while lifting up,
As down is down, and up is up.

Though down seems up, when upside down,
And up seems down, that way around,
Up is not down, down is not up,
As down is down, and up is up!

MARCH 20

DREAMS, DEEDS, AND DESTINY

Do you feel out of sync or out of place,
As if suspended, somewhere out in space,
Or at the mercy, of a fickle fate,
Either born too early, or born too late?

Do the things that once brought satisfaction,
Now cause discontent and aimless action?
And do you constantly, self-medicate,
Or shop till you drop, to lift your mind's state?

If you answered "yes", your life needs changing,
Conciliating, and rearranging,
So that it proceeds, harmoniously,
With your ever, evolving destiny.

While your destiny's set, to some degree,
It is not set unilaterally,
By the cosmos, or by your wants, and needs,
But it is fueled by, your dreams, and deeds.

So when you dream, do not dream, timidly,
And never dream dreams, narrow-mindedly,
But dream, bold dreams, with your mind open wide,
And with your destiny, be satisfied.

Your deeds, also fuel, they maximize,
Whether or not dreams, materialize;
So the fueling, of your destiny,
It falls squarely in, your authority.

However, you don't decide the details,
Concerning all, your destiny entails:
Thus your ever, evolving destiny,
In the main, it remains a mystery.

So with dreams, deeds, and the cosmos, daily,
Designing your evolving destiny,
Your life's tragedy is *not* that you die;
It's using fuel, too feeble, to fly.

Gwendolyn Rose Forrest

MARCH 21

DREAMS DEFERRED AND DREAMS DENIED

Ship foghorns blare out, warning blasts,
While train whistles warn, loud and fast,
And mourning doves, mournfully cry,
That dreams deferred too long, shall die.

Your dreams deferred, wait patiently,
To become your reality,
For dreams deferred, linger inside,
Before becoming, dreams denied.

And dreams denied, denied too long,
Definitely, they're dreams done wrong,
For dreams denied too long, inside,
Decay, and become dreams, that died.

MARCH 22

THE DUDES AND DOLLS

(For Claudia, my mother)

When the caller called, "I want each set squared,
A lady and gent, with each other paired,
Four couples to a set, to form that square,"
One set looked grand; the Dudes and Dolls were there.

All the Dudes were dressed, in silver and blue,
While the Dolls were dressed, in the same hues too;
No square dance club, looked finer on the floor,
And the Dudes and Dolls' hopes, started to soar.

The next call, "Dos-a-dos, like you can fly,"
Sent the strutting Dudes and Dolls, stepping high;
As the calls increased in complexity,
They executed each call, perfectly.

The Dudes and Dolls, were twisting, and twirling,
With Dolls' petticoats, swishing, and swirling;
Impassionedly, desiring to win,
The Dudes and Dolls danced their best, to the end.

The judges voted, and when they were done,
They declared that the Dudes and Dolls had won;
So do your best, to each endeavor's end,
Like Dudes and Dolls, and win or lose, you win!

MARCH 23

DUSK

When dusk descends, upon Paradise Lake,
Watercrafts depart, noise levels abate;
While daytime denizens, start settling down,
Nighttime denizens, start stirring around.

When dusk descends, upon Paradise Lake,
A peace descends too, that can heal heartache,
And when you forgive others, or yourself,
Peace descends, healing you, like nothing else.

MARCH 24

ENOUGH TIME

There is enough time, for you to do,
All of the deeds, belonging to you;
The other deeds must be left, undone,
As they belong to, another one.

Holding the enough-time point of view,
Controls the clock, and calendar, too,
Allowing you to enjoy as you,
Do all the deeds, belonging, to you.

Gwendolyn Rose Forrest

MARCH 25

EQUAL OPPORTUNITY

Think about equal opportunity.
Does it mean treat all identically?
Or does it mean equal access for all?
How do you interpret, the equal call?

Whether the former, and/or the latter,
This is not an esoteric matter;
To practice equal opportunity,
It benefits all of society.

MARCH 26

EVENTS

External events, you see with your eyes,
    Are seen with your mind, and with your heart too;
In other words, they are internalized,
    And interpreted from, an inside view.

So the way that events are classified,
    In the aftermath, of actual acts,
Is determined by what, you have inside,
    That's tinting, or tainting, the outside facts.

MARCH 27

EVER GREEN

Only the evergreen was seen,
A short time ago, wearing green;
Now winter has turned, into spring,
And green is seen, on everything.

The seasons spin, annually,
Turning us gray, gradually,
But when our zest for life, stays keen,
In essence, we stay, ever green.

MARCH 28

EXALTATION

I am an eagle! I can soar,
Beyond the bars, barring the door,
To my mind that was, heretofore,
Limiting, like a cage, and more.

I am an eagle! I explore,
Above the mountain, sea, and shore,
Where I have not explored, before;
Earth bound eaglet, I am, no more.

I am an eagle! And I fly,
Uninhibited, through the sky,
Exalting in pure ecstasy,
Experiencing life, love me!

MARCH 29

EXERCISE

In order to be physically,
    Healthy, hale, hearty, and fit,
You must exercise regularly,
    And bend your body, a bit.

Likewise, in order to exorcise,
    Your mind's negativity,
Your mind, you also must exercise,
    And do it, positively.

MARCH 30

EXPECT THE BEST

Thought fragments floating through Hank's head,
Came together, so that he read:
"Expect the best, from all you do,
For expectations do come true."

Thought re-fragmented, then reformed,
So that the same thought was reborn,
"Expect the best, from all you do,
For expectations do come true."

Crescendoing now, in Hank's head,
Thought climaxed, and aloud, he said:
"Expect the best, from all you do,
For expectations do come true."

No longer thought, but big and bold,
Understanding had taken hold:
"EXPECT THE BEST FROM *ALL I DO,*
FOR EXPECTATIONS DO COME TRUE!"

MARCH 31

EXTRAORDINARY

On a blustery day, at Anchor Bay,
The undulating waves wax blue, then gray;
They mirror the sky, containing a few,
Cumulus clouds, letting sunbeams stream through.

On a blustery day, at Anchor Bay,
The seagulls squabble, screech, scream, swoop, and play;
Scattering, then regrouping, as before,
They settle in the bay, and on the shore.

On a blustery day, at Anchor Bay,
Close to the shoreline a boy and dog play,
But because it is blustery, today,
Inside of vehicles, most people stay.

On a blustery day, at Anchor Bay,
At anytime, anyplace, any day,
Observation, of the ordinary,
Reveals life to be, *extraordinary!*

APRIL

APRIL 1

FACTS

Facts can be prioritized,
Analyzed and synthesized,
Catalogued and classified,
Counted and computerized.

Facts can be fictionalized,
Falsified and sanitized,
Till little is left intact,
To say a fact is a fact.

Kin to the wooded nickel,
When facts are proven fickle,
They fool us with fakery,
That feigns factuality.

Gwendolyn Rose Forrest

APRIL 2

FACTS OF LIFE

Gray clouds gathering, overhead,
Evoke a growing, sense of dread;
While Will likes driving, in the main,
He dislike driving, in the rain.

Yet despite his consternation,
To achieve his destination,
The following fact stands out plain:
Sometimes he must drive, in the rain.

Another fact, among life's facts,
Is life's mostly, repeated acts,
Acts like eating, and excreting,
All acts that require, repeating.

Done despite, or done willingly,
Most acts done, do undoubtedly
Make life less of a mystery;
These facts of life, keep mindfully.

APRIL 3

FAITH

Faith lets us amble out,
    Onto a busy street,
Undaunted, by the doubt,
    We'll be knocked off, our feet.

And when we are indoors,
    It's faith making the call,
That the ceilings, and floors,
    Will not crumble, and fall.

Planned or done, on a whim,
    The deeds we do, each day,
We would never, do them,
    Lacking, our faith's okay.

Faith propels us onward,
    And helps us follow through;
So on faith go forward,
    And make your dreams come true.

APRIL 4

FALLOW SEASONS

Everyone has his/her fallow seasons,
When he/she is fallow for these reasons:

To be ready for different seeding,
Periodically, we need weeding,
And for fertile seasons, to start again,
We must have fallow seasons, now and then.

APRIL 5

THE FAMILIAR

For over fifty years, Claudia's head,
Lay on the familiar, old-fashion bed,
With its fancy headboard, and footboard, too;
Both fashioned from wood, of a dark brown, hue.

Three of her children were conceived, in this bed;
Two of them, the world received, in this bed.
The bed witnessed, not only her desire,
But also witnessed, her husband, expire.

When reluctantly, she bought a new bed,
Everybody who saw it, quickly said,
"With its fancy headboard, and footboard, too,
This bed looks familiar, in style, and hue."

Often, before implementing, a change,
We may be reluctant, to rearrange,
That which is familiar, but when we do,
We find in the change, the familiar too.

APRIL 6

FATE

You had no say, in the way, you were formed,
Or in when, where, and to whom, you were born;
So are you the sole forger of your fate?
Or a robot which cannot deviate?

You are neither, but you must understand,
While you forge fate in the best way, you can,
By the dreams you conceive, and deeds, you do,
The universe forges your fate, *with you.*

APRIL 7

FEELINGS

If worthless is the way I feel,
    Actually, about myself,
Then worthless is the real deal,
    I feel about, everyone else.

Feelings, I project about me,
    Subconsciously, I turn into,
Feelings, no longer about me;
    They're about, ubiquitous you.

APRIL 8

FINAL ARRANGEMENTS

When I die, do not display my body,
For family, friends, and others, to see,
As I will not be in that cold, hard meat,
That the fire of life will not again heat.

Permanently passed on, from that purview,
I'll no longer be blood, bone, and tissue;
So don't plant my body in a grave, where,
You expect to come and visit me, there.

If I die without incident, quickly,
Donate organs, and cremate my body;
No need to maintain my ashes with care,
But have them dispose of, most anywhere.

Forget the flowers, and the funeral;
A brief memorial is optional,
And if a memorial's held for me,
Make the occasion celebratory.

Wear no black or white, dress colorfully,
And read my poem, "Immortality".
Sing secular songs, with an upbeat view;
Celebrate my life, and the life in you.

Lastly, allow me these final requests:
Make a donation to where you think best,
To where I specify, or plant a tree,
Please honor, final arrangements, for me.

Final arrangements can, and do vary,
For past one lifetime, flesh cannot carry;
Though the body is designed, wondrously,
It is designed for one lifetime, only.

But while the body loses all life, and lust,
And once again is recycled, into dust,
Cosmic power that empowered, the body,
It remains in existence, eternally.

APRIL 9

FIRE

The river was frozen solid,
Before the ball of fire arose,
And turned the river to liquid;
Now rapidly, the river flows.

Likewise transforming, love is fire.
Love turns loins, listless with cold,
Into infernos of desire,
That are the same for young, and old.

APRIL 10

FIREFLIES

Sam saw a flashing star,
  Falling toward the ground;
He sought that flashing star,
  But it could not be found.

Then Sam saw some fireflies,
  Flashing fast, in the dark;
So he sought the fireflies.
  Each was a tiny, spark.

Soon Sam caught some fireflies,
  Trapping them in a jar,
And he made these fireflies,
  His so called, flashing star.

But sadly, the fireflies,
  Denied their freedom, died,
Bringing tears, to Sam's eyes;
  So he sat down, and cried.

Loved ones are like fireflies;
  They need to fly, freely.
If too tight, are our ties,
  They leave, ultimately.

APRIL 11

FIRST STEP

The first time you espy, the star,
A dream beckoning, from afar,
Its allure, you'll likely deny,
Thinking it is too far, and high.

Although unsure, and full of fear,
With course uncharted, and unclear,
If this star allows you, no rest,
Determine to take up, the quest.

The first step you take into space,
Your doubts to conquer, fears to face,
Rallies the universe around,
To prevents you plummeting down.

The first step, you take from afar,
In an instant, transforms the star,
From dream, to possibility,
That can be a fait accompli.

APRIL 12

FLOW

Yesterday, the river was flowing fast,
But today, the river's as smooth as glass.
One day it flows rapidly, to the sea;
The next day it flows, imperceptibly.

Like the river, life flows fast, and flows slow,
In a straight line, or snaking, to and fro,
But wherever it goes, we must follow;
So why strive to arrive? Go with the flow.

When you strive to arrive, you just survive;
Going with life's flow, you survive, and thrive.
With striving, needs alone, are satisfied;
With flowing, needs and wants, are gratified.

So like a laidback, back-floating otter,
In a stream, of gently flowing water,
Relax! Be nonresistant to life's tow,
And with it, you will synchronously flow.

APRIL 13

FOCUS

Sailboats and sailboards, speedboats and jet skis,
Skim the lake's surface, with the utmost ease;
While the former forms of recreation,
Generate little reverberation,
The latter forms, with throttles open wide,
Generate a rousing, rip-roaring ride.

Adversities, at times, imitate these,
Reverberating speedboats, and jet skis;
Fueled by our focus, they roar around.
Cut fuel, and quickly, they quiet down.
Adversities cannot cause us, to dread,
When we focus on, what we want, instead.

APRIL 14

FOG

Fog, floating over the lake eerily,
Evokes a sense of insecurity,
But bright sunbeams, beaming through the fog make,
It frightening, as frosting, on a cake.

And fog is our phantom, free-floating fear,
That becomes benign, when courage draws near;
So if by courage, you let life be ruled,
By amorphous fog, you will not be fooled.

APRIL 15

FOLLOW YOUR DREAMS

(For Jacqueline, my granddaughter)

Follow your dreams;
 Take one step, at a time.
In spite of what seems,
 Continue to climb.

You can overcome claims,
 Of cannot be,
To manifest the aims,
 You want to see.

But none of this is,
 To be accomplished,
If dreams stay wishes,
 Only half-finished.

So follow your dreams,
 Till they crystallize,
And turn into dreams,
 That you realize.

Follow your dreams,
 And to them, remain true,
Because your dreams,
 Define your life, for you.

APRIL 16

FOR WHOM

Whenever the living gasp, their last breath,
From earthly concerns, they are freed, with death;
They don't wait around, somewhere in the sky,
To greet the living, when the living, die.

When loved ones die, for whom is it, we mourn?
Is it the dead, who have shed burdens borne?
Or is it the living, for whom, to cry,
Bearing the burden that they too, must die?

So for whom do we cry, when loved ones leave?
For neither the dead, nor the living, please,
But mourn time lost with the dead, when they die,
And give thanks for time with them, when you cry.

APRIL 17

FORGIVE AND FORGIVE

Release retribution, and resentment,
For retained, they boil, bubble, and ferment,
Then harden, holding you in past cement,
That keeps you from living, in the present.

So choose to use, your power, to forgive,
Others, and yourself, so that you may live,
Unrestrained by resentment, or regret;
Forgive and forgive, until you forget.

But anything, not in your interest,
In it, by no means must you, acquiesce.
Forgive and forget, so freely you live;
If you can't forget, forgive and forgive.

APRIL 18

A FORK IN LIFE'S ROAD

So you dreamed of success, and happiness,
Then did your best, to make them manifest,
When from out of a brilliant, bright blue sky,
A devastating tsunami dropped by.

Now with your dreams wholly in disarray,
You're afraid you cannot regain, your way,
And your dreams are too heavy, of a load;
You have arrived at, a fork in life's road.

When a fork in the road of life, is met,
Do you have to give up the course, you've set?
No, if you hear your heart, and let it steer,
A fork in life's road cannot make you veer.

Gwendolyn Rose Forrest

APRIL 19

FORMULA FOR SUCCESS

Within sight of your mind's eye,
    Within reach of your hands too,
Neither too far, nor too high,
    Success is waiting for you.

So don't just wish upon a star,
    Or to your meager means, kowtow,
But do your best, right where you are,
    With *whatever* you have, right now!

APRIL 20

FORTUNE

If you crack a fortune cookie,
    To find where your fortune, will lead,
The fortune found in the cookie,
    Will not be the fortune, to heed.

The fortune found in the cookie,
    Was created by someone else;
So yours is not in the cookie.
    You create your fortune, yourself.

Gwendolyn Rose Forrest

APRIL 21

THE FUTURE

Do not flinch from the future,
　　While pining after the past;
The past holds a false allure,
　　For the past can't be re-casted.

Do not favor the future,
　　Over the day, you now see.
The present day is for sure;
　　The future is a maybe.

And do not fear the future,
　　Thinking it is all unknown,
For fruit reaped in the future,
　　Is seed that today, you've sown.

APRIL 22

THE GENERATION GAP

The generation gap between,
Parent and child is often seen,
As it's a recurring schism,
That creates antagonism.

The generation gap's a breach,
But not, an unreachable reach,
For generations have not found,
This gap's too great, to reach around.

Gwendolyn Rose Forrest

APRIL 23

GENEROSITY AND RECIPROCITY

This adage is well-known:
    You will reap what, you sow.
If apple seeds are sown,
    Then apple trees will grow.

The same holds true, for fleas,
    For fleas beget more fleas;
Likewise, the bumblebees,
    Beget more bumblebees.

If for tree, flea, and bee,
    This adage does hold true,
For generosity,
    It must do the same, too.

But generosity,
    It's only half, the act;
Receiving graciously,
    It puts the rest, intact.

When receiving graciously,
    Meets giving generously,
Then giving generously,
    It reaps reciprocity.

APRIL 24

GET A GRIP

Do you long to live like celebrities,
Who seem to live "the good life" as they please?
And do you believe your life is blasé?
If so, you're letting your life, slip away.

Everyone's life is an uneven trip,
With many twists and turns, ascents and dips;
So don't let yourself be vacuumed into,
The vortex of someone else's, purview.

It is crucial for you, to understand,
The joystick of life, you hold in your hand,
But out of your hand, this joystick will slip,
If on your *own* life, you don't, get a grip!

Gwendolyn Rose Forrest

APRIL 25

GIVE BIRTH

Don't plant your organs,
    Inside of a grave;
Instead, create plans,
    To assist or save,
        Life, as of these plans,
            There exists a dearth.
        Donate your organs,
            And thereby, *give birth.*

APRIL 26

GOOD, BETTER, AND BEST

It is good to be wise, also wealthy,
But better to be happy, and healthy;
Yet the best to be, indubitably,
It is happy, healthy, wise, and wealthy.

APRIL 27

GRACE

Glen met an old woman, whose name was Grace;
Her words he remembered, if not her face.
In every season, most days of the week,
She retold this story, at Stony Creek:

"My husband, who passed on, some time ago,
Liked to fish at Stony Creek, and although,
I did not like to fish, or to clean them,
I did like to come to this park, with him."

"Now rather than watching daytime, TV,
Or visiting neighbors, excessively,
I come to the park, most days of the week,
And still enjoy myself, at Stony Creek."

Advanced age is a period of grace,
A period, much too precious, to waste;
So whatever it is that makes you sing,
During your grace period, DO YOUR THING!

APRIL 28

GRATITUDE

Your gratitude makes a good gift,
For it is guaranteed to lift,
Both giver and receiver's mood,
Into a lofty attitude.

Gratitude also, makes good sense,
By doubling up, the consequence,
And lifting two, not just one mood;
So give the gift, of gratitude.

APRIL 29

GRAY

The sky is overcast, today,
Showing several shades, of gray;
Mirroring it, in every way,
The lake, likewise, looks gray, today.

Whenever there is so much gray,
It's hard to keep the blues, at bay;
So remember, on a gray day,
Wear bright colors. Do not wear gray.

.

APRIL 30

GREEN SPACE

There is a mystic quality,
About green space, in the city,
That attracts with a strong allure;
Just what lures us, we are not sure.

Perhaps, it is the peaceful pace,
Perceived, inside of a green space,
With a pretty fountain, or pond,
Of which, we're especially fond.

Regardless, midst concrete, and steel,
Green space exudes nature's appeal;
So it would be such, a pity,
Were no, green space, in the city.

MAY

MAY 1

GRIEF

Do not grieve, due to some,
    Untrue egregious act,
That to your mind did come,
    From your ego, in fact,
        But an act, you presumed,
           Came from another's mind;
        This type grief, when assumed,
        It's the lingering kind.

So whenever you grieve,
    (And grieve, sometimes you must,
Such as, when loved ones leave,
    And return to the dust),
        Suffer curative grief,
           Which heals, and then moves on,
        For life is much too brief,
        To let grief, linger on.

MAY 2

GROW YOUR CREATIVITY

Every time that you unleash,
    Your innate creativity,
You cause it not to, just increase,
    But increase, exponentially.

So grow your creativity;
    Don't go about, suppressing it.
Expand it exponentially,
    By going out, expressing it!

MAY 3

GUARDIANS

Earth's creatures living everywhere,
Have been entrusted to our care;
Whether they walk, swim, fly, or crawl,
We are guardians, of them all.

So agribusinesses, understand this:
Animals feel pain; they are not widgets.
Callously using engineering skills,
For profit, inhumanely maims then kills.

We are arrogant, to assume,
We can, without costs, cause their doom,
When we destroy their habitat;
We are guardians too, of that.

So let's respect them, as they are,
And share resources, near and far;
Earth's creatures we cannot create,
But we can help them procreate.

So it's our challenge, one and all,
To help them walk, swim, fly, or crawl,
In a natural habitat,
And that is all there is to that!

MAY 4

GUSTS

Today displays both sunshine, and shower,
With wind gusts above, twenty miles per hour,
Causing scudding clouds, covering the sun,
To be fast replaced by another, one.

Gusting steadily, through the top of trees,
Wind gusts bend tree tops back and forth, with ease;
They make kids with kites fight with them, to play,
And the rivers run rapidly, today.

Whipped up by wind gusts, whitecaps run a race,
With sturdy sailboats sailing at a pace,
While less sturdy sailboards, sightly but slight,
They're buffeted about, because they're light.

Wind gusts, not only, whip up the water,
But whip at joggers, who fail to falter,
Which shows us, when we're whipped at, by life's gusts,
If we fail to falter, life won't, whip us!

MAY 5

HABITS

Habits require repetition to form,
But once they are formed, they become, the norm;
They put us on automatic pilot,
And this makes us behave, like a robot.

Habits work for us, or work against us:
So they can be a plus, or a minus;
They keep us, vigilantly, on our toes,
Or they cause us, many unwanted woes.

And habits do not change, out of the blue;
However, there is something, we can do.
We can change the habits that, we acquire,
By repeating behavior, we desire.

MAY 6

THE HANDS OF TIME

On the unseen clock of eternity,
The hands of time turn, continuously;
Yet the future is mainly, mystery,
And the past remains merely, memory.

Memory may paint the past ideal,
With what is remembered being unreal;
Though memory may change, the past in mind,
It can never turn back, the hands of time.

The hands of time turn, and life does unfold;
The young don't stay young, but become the old.
Turning, turning, in an eternal clime,
Forever turning, are the hands of time.

So we would be wise, to live in the now,
The only time we live in, anyhow,
And we must acknowledge, in our life-climb,
Out of our control, are the hands of time.

MAY 7

HAPPINESS

Happiness causes your heart rate to ease,
  And your body to feel good, through and through;
It gives you an attitude, sure to please.
  So health-wise, happiness is good, for you.

In people, places, and/or possessions,
  You may search for it, but it, you'll not find;
Independent of booms, or recessions,
  Happiness is solely, a state of mind.

No matter what is done, or what is said,
  You decide, what your state of mind will be;
So create some happiness, in your head,
  By making up your mind, to be happy.

Then try to be happy, most of the time;
  If you do this, in no time you will find,
That for the remainder, of your lifetime,
  Happiness is mainly, your state of mind.

MAY 8

HAZE

Thick as pea soup, haze hides the distant shore,
Giving the view that, the shore is no more,
When bright sunbeams stream through the haze, and make,
A sunlit path, and it crosses the lake.

Worry is a haze that hides from your eyes,
The sunlit path, you would see otherwise,
Leading you out of, adversity's maze,
Were you not hoodwinked, and hassled, by haze.

MAY 9

HEAD CHATTER

Your participation, in head chatter,
Does not make you mad as, the Mad Hatter;
These conversations, you have with yourself,
They are meant for you, and nobody else.

And head chatter makes you feel glad, or sad;
It also makes you behave good, or bad.
As in your head, there's a constant patter,
Always be aware of, your head chatter.

When your head chatter gets out of control,
Upon your life, this takes a heavy toll;
So since what's said, in your head, does matter,
Remain in control of, your head chatter.

MAY 10

HERE AND NOW

Here and now, is the right time to find,
Prosperity, along with peace of mind;
Yesterday's tomorrow is here, today,
And likewise is, tomorrow's yesterday.

So here and now, is the right time to give,
Yourself unto life, so that you can live,
In the way, your destiny does allow;
In other words, live your bliss, *here and now!*

MAY 11

HERE AND THERE

If, like meteors, we could range,
 Among distant stars, and their lot,
The following fact would not change:
  We cannot go where, it is not;
   In space, as on earth, everywhere,
   Cosmic power is here and there.

So when upon us, death does call,
 Dislodging our last breath of air,
Cosmic power leaves not at all,
  Because it exists everywhere;
   In death, as in life, and fore'er,
   Cosmic power is here and there.

MAY 12

HEROES AND HEROINES

Are all the heroes and heroines gone,
And all heroic deeds already done?
When somebody conquers a fear or doubt,
That's what most heroic deeds are about.

So heroes and heroines are not gone;
With little or no fan-fare, they go on,
Doing for the denizens, of the earth,
Unheralded deeds, of which there's no dearth.

.

MAY 13

HIGH ON LIFE

Whenever you feel weighted down,
Unable to get off the ground,
And you want relief, from your plight,
Getting high on life makes you light.

You do not need intoxicants,
Or artificial stimulants,
To lift you, so you can take flight;
Getting high on life, gives you height.

With all your faculties, intact,
Unclouded, not shrouded, in fact,
You can live, with all of your might.
Getting high on life is *all right!*

MAY 14

THE HIGHWAY OF HAPPINESS

No, the Highway of Happiness,
    It's not the same as Easy Street,
Though the Highway of Happiness,
    And Easy Street, sometimes, do meet.

Yes, the Highway of Happiness,
    Forces you to face doubts and fears,
For the Highway of Happiness,
    It crisscrosses the Trail of Tears.

MAY 15

HOME

All around the world, it is known,
    From Rwanda, Rio, to Rome,
That shared with someone, or alone,
    Everyone needs a place called home.

Inside, of a house, walls are found,
    But walls aren't found, inside, a home;
Instead, these qualities abound,
    In quantity, from base, to dome:

Beauty, courage, love, faith, freedom,
    Happiness, hope, health, harmony,
Safety, order, trust, truth, wisdom,
    Peace, along with, prosperity.

A home is for its residents,
    Much more than a place, to reside;
A home is for its occupants,
    All the qualities found, inside.

Gwendolyn Rose Forrest

MAY 16

HOMELAND

While the spinning, we neither sense, nor see,
We're spinning in space, continuously,
On a blue body, we call Planet Earth,
And it's our homeland, where we make, our berth.

Yet our homeland's not ours, to inherit,
As our ancestors have never, owned it;
At our birth, Planet Earth, we just borrow,
Until to earth, we return, tomorrow.

While on the earth, rain falling from the sky,
Replenishes our fresh water supply,
Fracking poisons the water that, we drink,
And in due time, it will make us, *extinct!*

Consequently, for all that, it is worth,
Let us preserve, our homeland, Planet Earth,
By making all anti-conservation,
Acts taboo, in each and every nation.

MAY 17

HOPE

Are you hanging at the end, of your hope?
Well do something more than hang there, and mope;
Before you plummet into hopelessness,
Summon to mind, a previous success.

Now cling to this, till you're able to climb,
Back into a more optimistic clime.
Hope is the rope hanging o'er hopelessness;
So reinforce hope, with thoughts of success.

Gwendolyn Rose Forrest

MAY 18

HORIZONS

The earth's horizon seems real, to the eye,
But it is an illusion, earth meets sky;
When we try to reach the earth's horizon,
It retreats, and we chase it, to no end.

Concealing what lies beyond, from our view,
It would have us believe all ends, with it too;
While beyond earth's horizon, we can't come,
Beyond does go on, *ad infinitum.*

The future is another horizon;
It hides, what lies, beyond the present's bend.
Privy to the present, primarily,
For us, the future's mainly, mystery.

Likewise, the future is an illusion,
For when we approach it for intrusion,
It retreats, and we chase it, to no end;
Seldom do we see past, the present's bend.

Chasing after an illusion, in haste,
It's a waste of time too precious, to waste,
And as it's an act, at which we can't win,
It is futile, to chase, a horizon.

MAY 19

HOW WE SEE THE SEA

We went to see, some whales at sea,
But whales at sea, we did not see;
Yet we did see, exclusively,
The sea, the sea; this we did see.

When we did see, whales suddenly,
The whales the sea, swallowed swiftly,
And we did see, once more only,
The mighty sea; this we did see.

The sea we see, we trash freely;
Yet on it we, depend daily.
Change how we see, the sea quickly,
Or with the sea, we'll die surely.

MAY 20

HUMANS BEINGS AND OTHER THINGS

Honey, a teddy bear, is play-mother,
To Tawny Bear, and her baby brother,
That befittingly is called Brownie Bear,
Because his coat is chocolate not fair.

Both Honey and Tawny, wear a bonnet,
But Brownie's head bears, no bonnet, on it;
Instead, he wears a bonnie blue sweater,
His humans believe, makes him look better.

Through the ages, in all societies,
We've personified beasts, and deities;
Personifying non-human beings,
Concedes we're connected, to other things.

MAY 21

IDEAS

Ideas are archetypical things,
    Containing latent power to create,
Other ideas, and objective things,
    When, they are projected, past the mind's gate.

And ideas, we accept to express,
    They're activated, immediately;
So when we add our deeds, to this process,
    Ideas become a reality.

Gwendolyn Rose Forrest

MAY 22

ILLUSIONS

The night creates the illusion,
    That the sun is forever gone,
While the morning in collusion,
    Seems to, restore the sun at dawn.

The creek creates the illusion,
    Of running on course rapidly,
When it is a frozen fusion,
    Of, crystallized, ice imagery.

The bird creates the illusion,
    Of being unable, to fly,
Causing predators, confusion,
    And this keeps fledglings flying high.

And you create the illusion,
    Of being that which, others see,
When, in fact, you are not yet done;
    You're an unfolding mystery.

MAY 23

IMAGINATION

Formless and as free as the breeze,
Recognizing, no, boundaries,
Imagination takes us far;
Unused, it leaves us where we are.

So use, your imagination,
To infuse, your life with passion,
And live a life that is inspired,
Not, in mediocrity mired.

Gwendolyn Rose Forrest

MAY 24

IMMORTALITY

Let the life I live,
    Be a life of worth;
Let it live to give,
    And be good, for Earth.

When the life in me,
    No longer does live,
Via memory,
    Let my life still give.

And when memory,
    Fades, till it is gone,
In lives yet to be,
    Let my life, live on.

Let the life I live,
    Live on after me,
And to me, thus give,
    Immortality!

MAY 25

IMPRESSIONS

Impressions in the sand, vividly show,
That across the beach, somebody did go,
Beyond the cabana, stripped white, and blue,
And here, the impressions vanish, from view.

Some people, like impressions in the sand,
Come into your life, for just a short span,
And leave impressions, remaining, in view,
Long after, they've vanished from, your milieu.

MAY 26

THE "IN CROWD"

Rather than rational beings,
We are emotional beings,
Who, rationalize emotion,
Then defend this, with devotion.

Accepting armed conflicts, and wars,
As proper means, for settling scores,
We price human life, less than pride,
And slyly sanction genocide.

Mixing our myths, with facts, and fear,
To absurdities, we adhere,
While ethnocentric traditions,
We can't see their contradictions.

ETHNOCENTRISM IS PASSÉ!
No longer can it rule today;
In a global community,
The "In Crowd" is humanity.

MAY 27

IN DUE TIME

In due time, spring springs, in light greenery;
Then summer darkens, spring's bright, scenery.
Later, fall falls, multi-coloring all;
After which, winter whitewashes, the fall.

In due time, seasons come, and seasons go;
Their pace, we can neither speed up, nor slow,
Nor can we speed up, or slow destiny;
So why strive to arrive?   Live leisurely.

Gwendolyn Rose Forrest

MAY 28

IN LOVE'S DOMAIN

There are so many lovers,
With hair of silver and gray;
Oblivious of others,
They saunter beside the bay,
Or dine in fine restaurants,
Conversing intimately,
Or they frequent fancy haunts,
And enjoy the revelry.

There are so many lovers,
With hair of silver and gray,
Behaving like young lovers,
In each significant way,
That this conclusion is plain,
And not shortsighted, but sage:
Wisely so, in love's domain,
Of no importance is age.

MAY 29

INNER SANCTUM

When you are unsure, and your fears abound,
You do not need anyone else, around,
Muddying the waters, blurring your views,
As they befuddle you, with *their* issues.

Instead, what you need is a private place,
So you can commune, in a sheltered space,
That's located not far away, but near,
Where peace prevails, and perception is clear.

You may travel, the whole wide world around,
But in no other places, can be found,
The peace promoting mental clarity,
Your inner sanctum offers you, for free.

Gwendolyn Rose Forrest

MAY 30

INSIGHTS

An insight starts as a small light,
Flickering until it grows bright,
Into a strong, and steady sight,
Exciting in us, such delight,
That imagination takes flight,
Igniting, another, insight.

MAY 31

INTERLUDES

Life's periodic interludes,
They are lulls, in our habitudes,
That upon our evolving fate,
Give us the time, to concentrate.

And interludes, planned or unplanned,
Used beneficially, sure can,
Make mundane, meager existence,
Become lifelong, efflorescence.

JUNE

JUNE 1

INTERNAL TIME

The clock allots time, tick-tock by tick-tock,
But your time's not allotted, by the clock;
The calendar allots time, day by day,
But your time's not allotted, in this way.

So place no stock, in calendar, or clock;
To let them allot your time is to mock,
The way you allot time, internally.
As your own timepiece, you are more, timely.

So let those pressed-for-time thoughts, unneeded,
Pass in and out of your head, unheeded,
And you'll have time, to enjoy, while you do,
All of the deeds, that are your deeds, to do.

It is possible, in the space-age world,
With all its pressure about time, awhirl,
To resonate with the rhythm, and rhyme,
That is in sync with, your internal time.

JUNE 2

INTUITION

My intuition compels me,
To include in my life journey,
Consequences, I can't foresee,
While of others, it forewarns me.

At my beck and call, hour on hour,
Intuition's cosmic power,
And when from it, I don't cower,
My best interest does flower.

While I can't empirically,
Show how it works, from A to Z,
I do know this, with certainty;
My intuition works for me.

JUNE 3

JOURNEY

We may journey together, for a while,
Sharing a secret, a sob, or a smile,
But to find out what life is all about,
Each one must journey on a solo, route;

No parent, child, spouse, sibling, or other,
Can journey the same route, as another;
Traveled by one person, exclusively,
Everyone's life is a solo journey.

JUNE 4

JOY

Joy is a gushing, geyser,
Originating inside,
And as joy is no, miser,
It gushes high, and spreads wide.

No man, woman, girl or boy,
Can end the joy that's, in you;
Only you can end the joy.
That begins and ends, with you.

As joy is hard to contain,
It will overflow its cup;
In the sunshine, or the rain,
Joy stays ready to erupt.

JUNE 5

JUDGING OTHERS

To the red bird, the blue bird said,
"Real birds aren't red, but blue, instead."
Shaking his head, the red bird said,
"You're mistaken, real birds are *red!*"

An old owl, asleep in the tree,
Awaken and growled, grumpily,
"Why are you birds, boisterously,
Bickering, and bothering me?"

Continued the owl, "Red or blue,
Birds are birds, regardless of hue;
So do not judge, by just one clue."
After so saying, off he flew.

Judging others, in ways, unjust,
Fosters injustice, and mistrust;
So let's not judge, but when we must,
As we want others, to judge us.

JUNE 6

JURISDICTION

The girl beheld the butterfly,
Scrutinizing it, eye to eye,
Pondering, while wondering why,
It did not spread its wings, and fly.

The butterfly beheld the girl,
Wondering why, in all the world,
Her wings, the girl did not unfurl,
And quickly fly off in a whirl.

What lies behind, another's eyes,
Without a doubt, would cause surprise;
That's why, only behind your eyes,
Is where, your jurisdiction lies.

JUNE 7

JUST AS YOU ARE

The spectacular daystar in the sky,
It's self-sufficient, nothing is awry;
Circulating on a course, far and wide,
The daystar carries a compass, inside.

Similar to the daystar in the sky,
You're self-sufficient; nothing is awry.
Circulating on your course, far and wide,
You also carry a compass, inside.

So if the course, you are on, currently,
Is not the course, on which, you want to be,
Consult your compass, for guidance, today,
And if need be, change your course, right away.

You have no reason, to delay the date,
Since you stay in a self-sufficient state;
Of equal importance, like the daystar,
You can begin to change, *just as you are!*

Gwendolyn Rose Forrest

JUNE 8

KALEIDOSCOPE

Trial and triumph, hopelessness and hope,
They're huge factors, in life's kaleidoscope,
And they are constantly changing places,
To provide us room, between the spaces,
For the promotion, and the pursuit of,
Life patterns premised, upon peace, and love.

The past has passed; the future's yet to be;
The present is our opportunity,
To mix lessons learned, and aspirations,
Experience earned, and expectations,
With the factors in life's kaleidoscope,
To create peace patterns, of greater scope.

JUNE 9

KIN

The wise wind whispers:
"Think of all others,
Either as sisters,
Or as your brothers;
Required by us all,
Birth, breath, and life's end,
They're making the call,
All people are kin."

JUNE 10

KNOWING

It's possible to believe, a falsehood,
　　But knowing is confined to, what is true,
And truth is no wishy-washy, can't, could,
　　If, but, would…maybe, might, should…or ought to.

Truth *is* and *is* with no regard for time,
　　Or space, or condition, or circumstance;
This makes knowing difficult, to define.
　　Yet it's easy to come by, in advance.

And knowing's no accident, or mistake;
　　It remains incorruptibly, intact.
So knowing is impossible to fake,
　　And on it, you can confidently act.

JUNE 11

LANTERNS

Little lanterns burning brightly,
    They are, in fact, fireflies in flight;
Lighting up daily, and nightly,
    Never do they cease to, delight.

And a lantern's burning brightly,
    Inside you, like fireflies, in flight;
Guiding you daily, and nightly,
    It leads you to, your heart's delight.

Gwendolyn Rose Forrest

JUNE 12

LAUGHTER

Present in limitless quantity,
Laughter is a ready remedy;
Ready to roll, for both old, and young,
Laughter stays on call, behind, the tongue.

.

JUNE 13

LEGACY

When humans are conditioned, to conceive,
    Of females as being, inferior,
And at the same time, brainwashed, to believe,
    Males are inherently, superior,
        Female debasement is the legacy.

When the young, unfazed by the fear of death,
    And a sense of their own mortality,
Are programmed, from birth, to give their last breath,
    To appease a warrior mentality,
        Perpetual war is the legacy.

When a few rule unilaterally,
    Denying to others, equality,
Then compassion cedes to brutality,
    Dehumanizing all humanity,
        And *depravity* is the legacy.

JUNE 14

LEISURE TIME LOCALES

Buzzing bugs, and sonorous songbirds,
Harmonize in tunes, too lovely for word,
While seventeen goslings, swim in a line;
Ma Goose is in front, Pa Gander's, behind.

Guys and gals on sailboards, glide gracefully,
Over blue-green water, rippling gently,
While in a kayak, covering the feet,
One person paddles to a private beat.

When Mr. and Mrs. Mallard, splash down,
Minnows in the shoals, dart and dash around,
But a leggy crane, standing near the shore,
Simply scans the scene, sizing up the score.

Without warning, turtles soaking up sun,
Noisily, strike the water, on the run,
Causing some cautiously, grazing deer,
To bolt into the woods, then disappear.

As toddlers and teens, play in the water,
On the beach, senior citizens saunter,
And oblivious to others, save one,
Enamored lovers embrace, in the sun,

Leisure-time locales, like this, everywhere,
Warrant our constant, conscious care,
To counteract litter, and pollution;
So pitch in, be part of the solution.

JUNE 15

LEOPARDS

Liz saw a leopard, lying on a limb,
And she was wholly terrified, by him;
She felt like fleeing, but held her ground,
Then looked again, no leopard could be found.

Figment fears are like leopards, in your life,
Causing you unwarranted, stress and strife;
But if you hold your ground, and face them down,
Like Liz, you will find, no leopards, around.

JUNE 16

LESSONS

Into each life, some rain must fall;
Adversity assails us all.
So do not wail and ask, "Why me?"
When assailed by adversity.

In it, there're lessons, you must learn,
Some easy, some hard, to discern,
But despite their difficulty,
These lessons are necessary.

So best the test, you'll undergo;
Learn life lessons, you need to know,
And be assured, when tests prove long,
Lessons learned, won't let you go wrong.

JUNE 17

LET GO!

There will be numerous times when,
We must let go, to start again;
Because known things, we must discard,
Letting go sometimes, may seem hard,

We tend to cling, to what is known,
And even after, we've been shown,
That what is known, has been outgrown,
Still we cling, for the known, *is known.*

Nevertheless, for us to grow,
We cannot cling; we must let go.
Life is not static, or stagnant,
And stuck in place, like a magnet.

Life is like a rippling river,
Flowing forward, now and ever;
So rather than resist its tow,
Relax, enjoy the ride. LET GO!

JUNE 18

LIFE IS

Life is some pleasure, and life is some pain;
Life is some leisure, and some work for gain.
Life is some caring, some hope, and some love,
And it's despairing, and soaring above.

Life is repetitive, and rational,
And it's erratic, and irrational;
With its own reasoning, rhythm, and rhyme,
Life is a mystery, most of the time.

JUNE 19

LIFE IS NOT WHAT IT USED TO BE

Life is not what, it used to be,
　　Nor was it, as you remember;
Summer is seen, differently,
　　When, summer's seen, from December.

Life is not what, it used to be;
　　Things have changed, since back in the day.
You are where you are, currently,
　　But where you are, you cannot stay.

So dust off dreams, of yesterday,
　　Held in abeyance, out of sight,
For life is giving you today,
　　To bring yesterday's dreams, to light.

JUNE 20

LIFE STORY

Everyone has a life story, to tell,
With parts, on which one does not like, to dwell;
Each story is poignantly personal,
For each is autobiographical.

So what is the theme, of your life story?
Is it one of trial, triumph, glory?
Or is it one of defeat, and despair?
Is it a tragic tale, going nowhere?

To change your life story, takes the right stuff;
It takes your dreams, but your dreams aren't enough.
To make a success, of your life story,
Add deeds, to dreams of, triumph and glory.

JUNE 21

LIFETIMES

Only once in a lifetime does one meet,
    Somebody who sets one's being, aglow,
And from the very first time these two greet,
    Each other eagerly, it is, as though,
    They knew each other, some lifetime, ago.

Attuned to one another, instantly,
    Without the use of words, both seem, to know,
The other understands, intimately,
    The secrets in his or her heart, as though,
    Such secrets were shared, some lifetime, ago.

Thinking the other is unlike others,
    Their feelings, like wildfire, flame, flair, and grow;
Shortly, these two are consonant lovers,
    Coalescing so completely, as though,
    They loved each other, some lifetime, ago.

Love is so strong, within the heart, and mind,
    When one lover dies, love does not follow,
But lives in the one, who is left behind,
    Feeling unequivocally, as though,
Their love will resume, some lifetime, to go.

Gwendolyn Rose Forrest

JUNE 22

LIMITLESS LOVE

Love has limitless elasticity,
Giving it limitless, capacity;
As a consequence, when under duress,
Love is unable to snap, under stress.

So do not limit your love, to a few,
As limited love will return, to you;
Limitless love, begets, a lot of love,
And a lot of love, you will partake of.

JUNE 23

A LOAF OF BREAD

Something is wrong, in prosperous countries,
Where most people eat, when and what, they please,
But avaricious acquiring runs wild,
Among those with an adequate lifestyle,
While malnutrition plagues those underfed,
Who're too poor to afford, a loaf of bread.

And something is wrong, in poorer countries,
Where most cannot eat, when and what, they please;
So children, women, and men go hungry,
With bloated bellies, and dysentery,
While they bury growing numbers, of dead,
As most, cannot afford, a loaf of bread.

Something's wrong, with the world economy,
Which encourages, gross inequity;
No longer can nations fail, to address,
How, to get the whole world, out of this mess.
Economic equity has to spread,
If *all* are to afford, a loaf of bread.

Gwendolyn Rose Forrest

JUNE 24

LOOKING BACK

Looking back, on your life, from there, to here,
The things you gave up, those you still hold dear,
The storms, you've weathered, the sunshine, you've seen,
Are you amazed, you are still, on the scene?

There were other ways, to have made your climb,
By not doing deeds, you did, at the time,
But had you not done, what you did, somehow,
Life lessons you've learned, you would not know now.

Nobody's life journey is free from fears,
Consequences earned, some smiles, and some tears;
So while you don't know, what tomorrow holds,
Look forward to it, as your life unfolds.

You can't change yesterday, in anyway,
But you do control deeds, you do, today,
So that looking back later, proud you'll be,
Of how, you made tomorrow's memory.

JUNE 25

LOVE AND DEATH

We who love, hope that love will force,
Death in due time, to change its course;
Though we hope death's course, love will change,
Death's course, love cannot rearrange.

Nevertheless, death's certain call,
Does not diminish love, at all;
Love is such a powerful force,
Not even death can change love's course.

JUNE 26

MAKING LOVE

Making love is breathing fresh air,
　　After holding your breath, too long;
Making love is daring to dare,
　　After not for reasons, all wrong.

Making love is drinking, your fill,
　　After having, an empty cup;
Making love is topping, the hill,
　　After, your arduous climb up.

Making love with one, you adore,
　　Satisfies you, down to your core,
Lifting you high, so that you soar,
　　And you want to make love, some more.

JUNE 27

MARATHON RACE

Life is an ongoing marathon race,
    Containing challenges, along the way,
Forcing you to find, your personal pace,
    And win your victories, day after day.

Approaching a milestone, with the course clear,
    Sometimes is when the course seems, the longest;
Ironically, when a milestone's near,
    The temptation to give up is strongest.

But if you give up, when challenged in life,
    Before completing, what you are about,
You do so because, you have become rife,
    With, incapacitating, fear and doubt.

The way you respond, to your fear and doubt,
    Determines whether, you will win, or lose,
For you have the option of pulling out,
    Of a challenge, at any time, you choose.

But hanging tough, when the going gets rough,
    It's what takes you across, the finish line;
Beginning is good, but it's not enough.
    In life's marathon, finishing, works fine.

JUNE 28

MASKS

Masks come in myriad shapes, and sizes,
In multiple designs, and disguises;
Masks also are behaviors, good or bad,
That can make us happy, or make us sad.

Masks are addictions, sickness, suicide,
Any affliction, behind which, we hide,
And masks are masquerading, as though true,
Until in reality, dreams come through.

JUNE 29

THE MEADOW OF YOUR MIND

(For Karen, my grandniece)

Wandering through, the meadow of your mind,
    Pause now and then, to carefully reflect,
On forgotten, unfulfilled dreams, you find,
    Still, in flower, after years of neglect.

Inside, the meadow of your mind's domain,
    Your deferred dreams do not die, right away,
But in the meadow of your mind remain,
    And they can be fulfilled, another day.

So start fulfilling deferred dreams, you find,
    Still flowering fresh, within your focus,
For dreams still in, the meadow of your mind,
    They are important, to your life's purpose.

JUNE 30

MEDITATION

By clearing the mind, of ought nots, and oughts,
Meditation quiets turbulent thoughts,
And to a profound, peaceful perspective,
It makes the adherent's mind, receptive.

To reach a state of mind alteration,
There are many forms, of meditation,
Necessitating no, medication,
Nor techniques, such as, sleep deprivation.

So let's teach our children, to meditate,
To acquire a higher consciousness state;
When meditation's done diligently,
It aids adherents, and society.

JULY

JULY 1

MELODY

The words you speak make up the melody,
That plays when you're in others' company,
And this melody is easily sung,
For it is poised at the tip, of your tongue.

Equally important, this melody,
Can create dissonance, or harmony;
So check each melody, before it's slung,
So glibly off of the tip, of your tongue.

JULY 2

MEMORIES

(For Lou, my love)

When mesmerizing memories,
Come into my mind, as they please,
Current realities, I find,
Completely vanish from, my mind.

A love song on the radio,
Playing softly in stereo,
Summons up memories, of you,
And these are as fresh as, the dew.

Like Savannah, in the summer,
Smoldering hot, as an ember,
They relay a steamy story,
Of love shared, in all its glory.

The earth has spun, in countless turns,
And for you still, my body burns;
Your presence, scent, sound, taste, and touch,
Oh how I yearn for them, so much.

Although my present fantasies,
Get mixed up with my memories,
The following fact remains true:
I've loved no one, like I've loved you.

Extinguishing my earthly fire,
Will extinguish earthy desire,
And along with my love, for you,
It will end, my memories, too.

Memories, falling like timber,
Evoke feelings, we remember,
And at unexpected, moments,
We relive momentous, events.

.

JULY 3

MENTAL MUSIC

(For Gary, my nephew)

Hear the big bass fiddle hum,
Humming hot, with every strum;
Humming loudly, and lowly,
It hums swiftly, and slowly.

Hear the vibrant vibraphone,
Riffing rhythms, clear and strong;
Riffing loudly, and lowly,
It riffs swiftly, and slowly.

Hear the smooth, saxophone wail,
Wailing out, a touching tale;
Wailing loudly, and lowly,
It wails swiftly, and slowly.

Hear the thrilling trumpet trill,
Trilling out thrill after thrill;
Trilling loudly, and lowly,
It trills swiftly, and slowly.

Hear the smoking hot drums heat,
Heating up, with every beat;
Beating loudly, and lowly,
They beat swiftly, and slowly.

Hear the sultry songstress, sing,
Scatting sweetly, "Ring-A-Ding;"
Scatting loudly, and lowly,
She scats swiftly, and slowly.

Six statuettes, all dressed up,
Soundlessly serve music up,
And the music that you hear,
It affects, more than your ear.

The mental music, you play,
In your mind, day after day,
Like a friend, or like a foe,
Lifts you high, or lays you low.

JULY 4

MERRY-GO-ROUND

Eventually, we all come around,
To riding again, the merry-go-round,
Where colorful chariots, can be found,
With, painted horses going up, and down.

Eventually, we all come around,
To riding again, the merry-go-round,
Like little children who're close to the ground,
And like to go around, and up and down.

Eventually, we all come around,
To riding again, the merry-go-round;
The topsy-turvy, turning upside down,
And roller coaster ride, we put them down.

Eventually, we all come around,
To riding again, the merry-go-round;
When our anatomical clock, winds down,
Our ride of choice is the merry-go-round.

JULY 5

MESSAGES

Know that the message, you send,
    Is delivered loud and clear,
But not by the one, you spin,
    When bending somebody's ear.

And the message that's received,
    From your talk, silly or sage,
It's not the message, believed;
    Deeds deliver *this* message.

Gwendolyn Rose Forrest

JULY 6

MIDNIGHT BLUE

When darkness descends to cloak you,
    In a mantle, of midnight blue,
And the moon is hidden from you,
    By clouds colored midnight-blue, too,
        Remember, behind their lining,
        The moon is still brightly shining.

So on thoughts tinted midnight blue,
    Do not dwell another moment,
But on thoughts, bright as the moon, do,
    Dwell, and allow these thoughts to vent;
        Moon-lit thoughts lift your attitude,
        And brighten a midnight-blue mood.

JULY 7

MILLSTONE OR MILESTONE

During the course of your moments,
You will label major events,
As a millstone, or a milestone,
And by this label, they'll be known.

You'll either be ground down, like grain,
Or you will rise, and walk, again,
To discover, after a while,
That you have walked, another mile.

Millstone, making your life, a mess,
Or milestone, marking, a success?
The choice is yours, and yours, alone,
Whether a millstone, or milestone.

JULY 8

MODEST GIVERS GIFTS

There're time modest givers wish,
    That they were able to bestow,
        Gifts, like the gifts of noble kings;
However, when they're unselfish,
    Their modest gifts together show,
        They too, accomplish noble things.

JULY 9

MORE AND MORE

Each day, you are more, than the day, before;
Thus day, after day, you are more, and more.
More than your discourse, dreams, deeds, or their sum,
You also are that which, you can become;
So don't pigeonhole or typecast yourself,
There's more of you to come, like no one else.

Gwendolyn Rose Forrest

JULY 10

MORE THAN

There is no doubt, you have a hand,
In the design, of your life plan,
Charting your course, across life's seas,
A plan you design, as you please.

The plan, although designed, by you,
By dreams, you dream, and deeds, you do,
It's subject to more than you plan;
The cosmos also plays a hand.

JULY 11

MOUTH AND MIND

Between your mouth, and your mind,
  There's an immutable link,
Such that at times, you will find,
  Your mouth has spilled, what you think.

To avoid spills of this kind,
  Sending relationships, south,
Patrol and control, your mind,
  For your mind, controls your mouth!

Gwendolyn Rose Forrest

JULY 12

MUCH MORE

You are much more, than a full head, of hair,
Just as you would be, if your head, was bare;
Thoughts you think, words you speak, and deeds you do,
These are the meaningful things, making you.

So whether you're dark, medium, or fair,
You are much more, than the skin that you wear;
Much more than any trait, you have, or miss,
You're of value for the fact, you exist.

JULY 13

MUSIC

Like beauty is in the eye, of the perceiver,
So is music in the ear, of the receiver;
Thus a cacophony, displeasing to, one ear,
It's a sweet symphony, for another, to hear.

So why is it that we are musically bent?
Our preference in music is no, accident;
It's the music, we matured to, back in the day,
That's the music, we still prefer to hear, today.

Gwendolyn Rose Forrest

JULY 14

MUST DOS

(For Marie and Kay, my sisters)

Before each association meeting,
    Madam President had too much, to do;
It took more than a smile, and warm greeting,
    For her to see, each monthly meeting through.

The problems varied (some large, and some small),
    With most occurring, when least expected;
Whether with the speaker, or with the hall,
    Every problem had to be, corrected.

Once too often, Madam President was found,
    Before an association meeting,
Apologizing, and running around,
    Making sure guests had their proper seating.

Thereafter, before each monthly meeting,
    She sent out an email, which did begin,
"Members: Do less chitchatting, and greeting,
    And more, acting like, the Little Red Hen."

Like Madam President, you've "must dos" too,
    While those of others, are for them, to do;
Therefore, your primary "must do" is to,
    Discern the difference between, these two.

JULY 15

MYSTERY

More than sinew, blood, and bone,
　　More than molecule, or mind,
And while personally known,
　　It's difficult to define.

As a source of smiles, and sighs,
　　It is known, intimately,
To the owner, of the eyes,
　　And it's part of destiny.

Long before, the newborn, cries,
　　It begins where we can't see,
And when flames fade from, old eyes,
　　Life remains a mystery.

Gwendolyn Rose Forrest

JULY 16

A NAME

Regardless of fortune, or fame,
There is something about one's name,
That only the owner, can claim,
And only the owner, can shame.

This intangible quality,
It's the owner's identity;
While a name's a name, just the same,
A name is more than, just a name.

JULY 17

NEGATIVE THOUGHTS

When you make mountains, out of mole-hill things,
Negative thoughts, fervidly flap their wings,
And if too often, you fuss, fume, or fret,
Inside your head, hard like concrete, they set.

So how do you negate, negative thoughts,
The why mes, if onlys, can'ts, buts, and oughts?
To negate negative thoughts, in your head,
Replace them with positive thoughts, instead.

Gwendolyn Rose Forrest

JULY 18

NEVER ALONE

Life is such that you are ever, alone;
Nevertheless, you are never, alone.
If never alone, from cradle to shroud,
How are you ever alone, in a crowd?

All alone, you exist, concurrently,
With cosmic power in you constantly;
So in this way, you are ever, alone.
Nevertheless, you are never, alone.

JULY 19

NEW BEGINNINGS

If you plan to move,
   To new beginnings,
      Get unencumbered,
         Before, moving on,
Or take with your move,
   To new beginnings,
      Hang-ups you've incurred,
         To which, you hang on.

So be sure to tie,
   Up life's loose endings,
      And offenses mend,
         Before, moving on,
Lest loose endings vie,
   With new beginnings,
      On the horizon,
         Not able to dawn.

Gwendolyn Rose Forrest

JULY 20

NEW IDEAS

To solve the problems of today,
You cannot cling to yesterday,
As obsolete and stale precepts,
Cannot result in fresh concepts.

Intuition, intelligence,
Open-mindedness, common sense,
Will banish backward-facing fears,
And generate new ideas.

In winter, spring, summer, and fall,
In every season, one and all,
With new ideas to explore,
Come opportunities galore.

JULY 21

THE NEXT STEP

Whether you are a stupendous success,
Or a ne'er-do-well, with your life a mess,
At numerous times, during your lifetime,
You choose to continue, or cease to climb.

So regardless of which profile, you fit,
The climb of your life, you *de facto,* quit,
When you stay stuck, in a previous act,
And you fail to take the next step, *in fact.*

Gwendolyn Rose Forrest

JULY 22

THE NIGHT IS ALIVE

The night is alive with music,
Composed by creeping, crawling things;
If you listen, you can hear it,
Chirruping, buzzing, and humming.

The night is alive, with music,
Played on body parts, such as wings,
And we're amused by nature's wit,
Cause the insect orchestra, swings.

JULY 23

NIGHTFALL

When the copper-colored sun, hanging high,
Begins its descent, in the westward sky,
And eastward, dark shadows grow long, and tall,
This signals the commencement, of nightfall.

Nightfall begins the daily, turnaround,
Of diurnal denizens, settling down,
While nocturnal denizens start to stir,
When daylight dims, and dark shadows occur.

And nightfall is a good time, to reflect,
On the many ways, in which you connect,
With the cosmos, and everything in it,
To understand how in the world, you fit.

Gwendolyn Rose Forrest

JULY 24

NIGHTLIGHTS

From the darkened, distant skyways,
City streets, the country byways,
And bridges spanning, the river,
They sparkle, seeming to quiver.

Illuminating the dark night,
They curtail, or cast out, our fright;
Like the stars, luminous nightlights,
They incite in us, new insights.

JULY 25

NO LIMITS

Do not let apprehension,
    Concerning what the clan deems,
Conclude in the cessation,
    Of you, pursuing, your dreams.

When whatever, the clan deems,
    Causes you to cede, your plans,
The fulfilling of your dreams,
    It falls into others' hands.

The clan does not limit you;
    Limits are set, in your mind.
If to your dreams, you stay true,
    Then no limits, shall you find.

JULY 26

NO REGRETS

Regardless of how close to death, you are,
You still have today remaining, thus far;
So since life has not abandoned you yet,
Do not waste this time, in rue, or regret.

Instead, live today, as though it's your last,
Because possibly, this could come to pass,
But if you should live, for another, day,
You'll have no regrets, regarding, today.

JULY 27

NOT BY TASTE, TOUCH, SCENT, SIGHT, OR SOUND

From a tree, Gray Squirrel looked down,
And seeing no one else, around,
Dexterously, he darted down,
And he gathered nuts, from the ground.

In a short while, Gray Squirrel found,
Not by taste, touch, scent, sight, or sound,
That he was stalked, by a huge hound,
Which had stealthily, slunk around.

Wasting no time, scanning the ground,
Gray Squirrel, in a leap, and bound,
Dashed up the nearest tree, not down,
While the tree, the hound circled 'round.

Similarly, at times we've found,
Not by taste, touch, scent, sight, or sound,
Intuition is so profound,
When heeded, we're kept safe, and sound.

JULY 28

NOTIONS

A notion is precious, like a gemstone;
    So it must be mined, meticulously.
Also, it must be circumspectly honed,
    In order to, become reality.

So mine and hone, your notions, all alone,
    Within you, like secrets, you dare not share,
Until they are able, to hold their own,
    And not succumb, to the naysayer's snare.

JULY 29

A NUGGET OF KNOWLEDGE

A nugget of knowledge,
    Some people say,
Does not give an edge,
    Instead, leads astray.

But in books, or garbage,
    Waiting around,
A nugget of knowledge,
    It can be found.

And a nugget of knowledge,
    Gained, some way,
Becomes a huge hedge,
    That grows, day by day.

Once gained, a nugget of knowledge,
    Won't stray;
So gain, a nugget of knowledge,
    Today!

Gwendolyn Rose Forrest

JULY 30

OBLIVION

For a moment, we tread,
Life's tenuous, thin thread;
Into oblivion,
Must we continue on?

Do we cease, with our breath,
Extinguished, by our death?
Or do we, possibly,
Gain immortality?

If future lives are fed,
By the life, we have led,
Over oblivion,
We win, in the long run.

JULY 31

AN OCEAN

Life is an ocean, aqua and azure,
Undulating uninterruptedly;
About it, we can say just this, for sure:
Life's unpredictable, *predictably!*

One minute, it's calm, and the next, it churns,
While in advance, its moves, no one does know;
So with life's ups and downs, and twists and turns,
Do not fight, but be flexible, and flow.

AUGUST

AUGUST 1

ODE TO BELLE ISLE

Ships glide by Belle Isle, making little sound,
    Save for waves, in their wake, slapping the shores,
While smaller watercrafts, racing around,
    Drown nature's noise, in their riotous roars.

Seagulls scavenging triumphantly scream,
    Whenever, they make a successful, catch,
While seagulls stealing, triumphantly scream,
    Whenever, they make a successful, snatch.

A deer herd grazing, near a sheltered street,
    Seem unfazed, by the tarrying traffic,
While folks in cars, gazing at the deer eat,
    Think this sighting is simply, *fantastic!*

During daylight hours, Monday through Sunday,
    Belle Isle is a park, of youngsters, mothers,
Oldsters, and others, who feel nature's sway;
    After dark, it is a park, of lovers.

An island jewel, in Detroit city,
    Belle Isle beguiles for nature does beguile.
As nature's stewards, it is our duty,
    To preserve parks in cities, and the wild.

Gwendolyn Rose Forrest

AUGUST 2

OF BUNNY RABBITS, BUMBLEBEES, AND BOMBS

Bunny rabbits quiver, in the meadow,
    While pussy willows quake, beside the pond;
All of them sense, a sinister shadow,
    Hovering over that, of which they're fond.

And bumblebees buzzing, in the meadow,
    Buzz by people buzzing, beside the pond;
People buzz about bombs, about to blow,
    And nations denying, their common bond.

Prosperity can't grow, in the meadow,
    With bombs, and mines planted, beside the pond;
When around the world, peace is what we sow,
    The age of prosperity, will have dawned.

AUGUST 3

OF GRANDEUR

There is an air of grandeur,
About the goose, and gander,
While swaggering, to their bath,
That stops traffic, on their path.

And we've an air of grandeur,
Like that of goose and gander,
About us, when we forgive,
And magnanimously live.

AUGUST 4

ONE OF A KIND

(For Michael, my nephew – Happy Birthday)

Everyone is vulnerable,
    And no one is exempt, never.
Everyone is valuable;
    Do not discount yourself, ever.
.

Know you were born, with a purpose,
    Embedded in your heart, and mind;
So keep in focus your purpose.
    It's why you are one of a kind.

AUGUST 5

ONE RACE

Human inhabitants, of Planet Earth,
Too often discredit, each other's worth,
Citing pseudoscientific cases,
That claim we are of different races.

Formed from arbitrary biased, stories,
Capricious are these race, categories;
Varied cultural/physical faces,
Do not add up to, different races.

While humans do differ, on the surface,
All are members of a singular race;
And while of ethnicities, there're many,
All are the branches of only one tree.

Human seed is only that, *human seed;*
So with each other, we can, and do breed.
This fact alone makes a conclusive case,
There is only one race, the human race.

AUGUST 6

ONLY TODAY

Today is not the time,
To wait for tomorrow,
Nor is today the time,
To pine for yesterday,
For every tomorrow,
Is but an illusion,
While every yesterday's,
A foregone, conclusion;
So as only today,
Exists eternally,
It is only today,
That is reality.

AUGUST 7

OPEN SEASON

When females are targets for sex, and pain,
Who without costs, can be raped, maimed, and slain,
Because they lack rights, accorded to males,
It's always, open season, on females.

When thoughts, words, and deeds, and the law prevail,
Equally for the female, as the male,
Then the season of reason will begin,
And open season on females will end.

AUGUST 8

OPPORTUNITY

An opportunity,
    Knocks, only once some say,
But indubitably,
    It knocks, another day.

An opportunity,
    Thought lost, it can be found,
Dressed up differently,
    Next time, it comes around.

AUGUST 9

ORDINARY THINGS

Ordinary things,
Are picture-postcard pretty,
When seen with the heart.

Gwendolyn Rose Forrest

AUGUST 10

OUTCASTS

They push shopping carts, along city streets,
In search of something to sell, or to eat;
Living on the edge, of society,
They are those many stare at, but few see.

Forced to beg on streets, they endlessly roam,
These men, women, and children, with no home,
They're outcasts in space-age society,
Who, save for events, could be you, or me.

AUGUST 11

OUTCOMES

(For Tawnya, my niece)

As you don't know all, of the avenues,
    The cosmos determines, you will pursue,
Do not become distraught, thinking you lose,
    When outcomes you seek, seem not to seek you.

Your task is to choose, the outcomes, desired,
    And use, your ability to its best,
To change desired into outcomes, acquired;
    After which, the cosmos will do the rest.

AUGUST 12

PARADIGM SHIFT

"Cosmic power empowers you," Ruth read,
    While stumbling through the words that, she observed,
But in her mind, she heard these words, instead,
    "This theory is absolutely, absurd."

"Cosmic power empowers you," Ruth said,
    While mumbling through the words that, she now heard,
Reverberating, inside of her head,
    And mimicking her, like a mocking bird.

"Cosmic power empowers me, it's true!"
    However these words, were not what Ruth heard,
Yet in a profoundly wise way, she knew;
    For her, a paradigm shift had occurred.

This paradigm shift transmuted Ruth's view,
    Of the cosmos, unlike, anything else,
And cosmic power empowers you, too,
    But this paradigm, you must know, yourself.

AUGUST 13

PARENTS

People are imperfect parents,
    And as imperfect parents do,
They possess imperfect parents,
    And they've imperfect children, too.

Sometimes, the children hold a grudge,
    From the point of view, of a child,
But when mature, most children judge,
    In a manner that is, more mild.

Now they know imperfect parents,
    Like themselves, cannot help but be,
Imperfect people, who're parents,
    And people evolve constantly.

AUGUST 14

PARTS

Like kings, queens, and jacks, in a deck of cards,
It can be argued, you are only parts;
Your heart can be replaced, by another,
And most parts by some device, or other.

You lose a limb, or other parts, in fact,
But despite your loss, you remain, intact.
Essentially, an enigma, by far,
For more than your parts or their sum, you are.

AUGUST 15

THE PARTY

Pam hosted a party, the other day,
And all of her guests came prepared, to stay.
The first guests to arrive arrived, promptly;
They were Father Fear, and his wife, Worry.

Next Brother Blame came, with his girlfriend, Guilt,
And this duo was decked out, to the hilt;
Then Negative Thoughts came, with Double Doubt,
And this duo, likewise, was all decked out.

The party shifted into low gear, when,
What If, If Only, and Why Me, came in;
Now, Cousin Can't, and Aunt Anxiety,
Both began to party, most heartily.

When Uncle Uneasiness eased around,
To where Sister Sorrow was sitting down,
This made Woe-Is-Me, and Pity-Poor-Me,
Both begin to cry, conspicuously.

So by the time Bad Blues let down, his hair,
Pam was wallowing deep down, in despair;
She wallowed so deep she wished, she was dead,
Until this light-bulb moment lit up her head:

I am the party, giving the party,
However, it's not any fun, for me.
Instead, it is causing me such distress,
I want to get rid of, all of my guests.

253

Gwendolyn Rose Forrest

As soon as Pam conceived, the final thought,
In all of her guests, it instantly brought,
Feelings of foreboding, and of malaise;
So Pam spoke aloud, a positive phrase.

Soon thereafter, all her guests departed,
Leaving Pam feeling, very light hearted,
As though she had found, a four-leaf clover;
Without a doubt, the party was over!

If it is not, self-explanatory,
Here is the point, of this allegory:
The one a pity-party hurts the most,
It's not the invited guests, but the host.

AUGUST 16

THE PAST

Whenever the past is looked into,
It's looked into, from the point of view,
Of the reviewer; so it in part,
Reflects what's in, the reviewer's heart.

Yet if about the past, we don't know,
We won't know presently, where to go;
Lacking prior lessons, the past makes,
We are prone to repeat, past mistakes.

The past helps to put, in perspective,
How we've lived, and how we want to live;
With the good and bad, rolled into one,
The past is past; it's over, and done.

So let's put past lessons, we have learned,
With present wisdoms, we have discerned,
And letting the past, in the past stay,
Let's live, and let others live, today.

Gwendolyn Rose Forrest

AUGUST 17

PATIENCE

While into a tall tree, it waits to grow,
Patience aplenty, the palm seed does show;
Nestled inside of the nourishing earth,
Of patience, this snug seed displays no dearth.

To the passing of time, it pays no heed,
And preserves its potential, as a seed,
Till the day, it appears, under the sun,
No longer a seed; a tree has begun.

And the patience aplenty, we display,
Preserves our dream's potential, till the day,
It appears in full view, under the sun,
No longer a dream, but a deed, that's done.

AUGUST 18

PATTERN

There is a pattern, to which you conform,
A pattern that was, before you were born;
Consisting of innate, inclinations,
It is cause for tears, and celebrations.

Indelibly imprinted, upon you,
This pattern permeates, all that you do;
In your dreams, your deeds, and your destiny,
It's interwoven, intrinsically.

AUGUST 19

PAUSES

Pauses are pit stops, far away,
From the pursuits, of everyday;
They provide us time, to retool,
Refresh ourselves, and refuel.

On our short-term, and long-term fate,
They give us time, to contemplate,
And while they may be worried through,
Never, can they be hurried through.

Pauses are opportunities,
To assess possibilities,
And to deliberate, then choose,
To discard, any too-tight, shoes.

Pauses grant permission, to cut,
Out ego concerns, and to put,
Into the proper perspective,
How we live, and we want to live.

Pauses are prime times, to be pruned,
Of preconceptions, and harpooned,
By uncertainty, the unknown;
They're prime times to be shorn, and shown.

Lastly pauses, planned or unplanned,
Occur to help us understand,
While living out our destiny,
We are to live, purposefully.

AUGUST 20

PEACE SONG

If a few of us sing a peace song,
    A song promoting peace, in the world,
Soon many others will sing, along,
    And peace, in the world, will unfurl.

When enough of us sing, a peace song,
    While fine tuning, the dissonant part,
Peace in the world will become so strong,
    That war, in the world cannot restart.

Gwendolyn Rose Forrest

AUGUST 21

THE PENDULUM

The pendulum does swing,
　　Every generation,
And every swing does bring,
　　Reinterpretation,
Of societal forms,
　　And the transformation,
Of societal norms;
　　Every generation,
As it rearranges,
　　Current situations,
Stirs up other changes,
　　Fostering frustrations,
Within the preceding,
　　And post generations.
Ah, accord is fleeting!
　　Yet our consolation's,
While the pendulum's swing,
　　Brings disintegration,
The pendulum's next swing,
　　It brings integration.

AUGUST 22

THE PERSONAL PATH

The personal path, down through the ages,
Has been a path that awes, and amazes;
Without fail, it consistently does lead,
Past known paths, when the stout of heart take heed.

It's not a path, for the coward, or weak,
Nor is it one, the conformist would seek;
Once on this path, one cannot go backward;
The only option is to go forward.

Meandering through secret spaces where,
Personal discoveries are made there,
The personal path may be hard, to find,
But it's knowable, to the heart, and mind.

The personal path fans out, far and wide,
But its departure point begins, inside,
Of each of us, individually,
And each must search for it, personally.

The personal path, when all's said and done,
Is a path sought and trod, by only one;
So to fulfill, your unique destiny,
A personal pathfinder, you must be.

Gwendolyn Rose Forrest

AUGUST 23

PICTURES

The sun paints pictures, on the ground,
Of spreading shadows, at sundown,
While the luminous lunar light,
Paints shadow pictures, in the night.

And you paint pictures, in your mind,
By which, your life will be defined;
So in the pictures, you will live,
Paint a positive, perspective.

AUGUST 24

PLANET EARTH

Throughout the winter, spring, summer, and fall,
Planet Earth is the nurturer, of all;
Of every plant, animal, and person,
Planet Earth is the nurturer, bar none.

But Planet Earth's resources will not last,
With humans multiplying, much too fast;
To preserve resources, for all they're worth,
We humans must control our rate of birth.

Consequently, every human must play,
His/her family role, in such a way,
That for plant, animal, and human race,
Planet Earth remains a livable place.

AUGUST 25

PLANS AND PAUSES

More often than not, well-made plans,
    At some point will meet, with delay,
As even the best, well-made plans,
    Encounter pauses, in their way.

How well, with pauses, we contend,
    Decides how well, our plans will fare;
So do not let yourself descend,
    Down into doldrums of, despair.

Rather, keep on remembering,
    That despair and despondency,
(Not delay, and/or detouring),
    Are things, of which, to be wary.

Pauses in plans are not causes,
    For consternation, or concern,
For plans which have weathered pauses,
    Their validity has been earned.

AUGUST 26

PLEASENTRIES

A public park containing pleasantries,
It's a site in the city, sure to please;
In the park, a little log cabin lies,
But entry is granted, only to eyes.

While wind buffeting a weeping willow,
Cause her locks, to over the pond billow,
Inside the pond, a little lighthouse stands,
On one of several, little islands.

And frisky fish, breaching the pond's water,
Startle lovers, who by the pond saunter,
While small children smile at smaller ducklings,
Old men pitch horseshoes, play cards, and toss rings.

A home for nature, as well as beauty,
A public park, inside of the city,
Where we can play, or commune, as we please,
It's essential, as are its pleasantries.

AUGUST 27

PLEASURE AND PAIN

The things that induce,
    Within us, pleasure,
They also produce,
    Pain, in like measure.

Trailing each other,
    Like sunshine, and rain,
Tethered together,
    Are pleasure, and pain.

AUGUST 28

PLENTY

If you want plenty,
To fill in the blanks,
Think plenty, give plenty,
Give plenty thanks!

Gwendolyn Rose Forrest

AUGUST 29

PORPOISES

Wild whitecaps on the river, today,
Appear to be porpoises, at play,
Insouciantly, swimming upstream,
But things are not always, as they seem.

So it's not in our purview, to say,
That others are porpoises, at play,
When perhaps, they are struggling upstream,
In pursuit of an unfulfilled dream.

AUGUST 30

POSSESSIONS

If possessions, or lack,
　　Have you, obsessed,
By possessions, or lack,
　　You are possessed.

Of possessions,
　　You're not an extension;
Over possessions,
　　You have dominion.

So do not let possessions,
　　Possess you,
Or lack of possessions,
　　Do the same, too.

Gwendolyn Rose Forrest

AUGUST 31

POWER

Cosmic power in us, conquers with ease,
Our outer mountains, and inner valleys;
Like it does for the sun, daily, at dawn,
And the salmon swimming upstream, to spawn,
It empowers us also, to persist;
Upon staying our course, it does insist.

Indubitably, indomitable,
Unquestionably, unconquerable,
Cosmic power in us, consistently,
Coaxes and coaches us, to victory;
So in times of chaos, or of quiet,
Confide in it, and staunchly, stand by it.

SEPTEMBER

SEPTEMBER 1

PRAY NO PITY-POOR-ME PRAYER

Say thanks, prior to receiving,
That which you need, while believing,
This is a self-fulfilling, act,
And it fulfills itself, in fact.

Express gratitude, in your speech,
And do not bargain, or beseech;
In the cosmos, your needs are known,
Before to you, they have been shown.

So conceive an affirmation,
Expecting, manifestation,
And pray no pity-poor-me prayer;
Say thanks, before, fulfillment's there.

Gwendolyn Rose Forrest

SEPTEMBER 2

PREDICTIONS

When the cicadas' buzzing song,
Fills up the airwaves, before long,
We wonder why, all of the fuss,
And pose reasons, for the ruckus.

In the cicadas' buzzing song,
They are predicting, before long,
The summertime will be ending,
As autumn has its beginning.

And the cicadas' buzzing song,
Is predicting that, before long,
Your summer will be ending, too,
As your autumn, makes its debut.

So the cicadas' buzzing song,
Also implores that, before long,
In your autumn, you will explore,
Life unlike, you have done before.

SEPTEMBER 3

THE PRESENT

The present unseals,
   The lid on life's lot,
      The future concealed, yesterday,
And thereby reveals,
   The part of the plot,
      We performers perform, today.

The present, too, heals,
   The wounds the past wrought,
      That seemed to be with us, to stay,
And thereby it yields,
   Enjoyment that's brought,
      About by deeds, we do, today.

SEPTEMBER 4

PRIMARY PARENT

A child has physical parents, of course,
But they are not the child's primary source.
While this is not readily apparent,
The universe is primary parent.

This makes sisters of daughters, and mothers,
While making fathers, and their sons, brothers;
Though physical parents, can propagate,
Only the universe originates.

SEPTEMBER 5

PRIORITIES

Maladies, such as AIDS and Ebola,
Plaguing many countries, in Africa,
And menacing, many other countries,
Need not be mortifying, maladies.

But resources are waylaid, to wage war,
Instead of used, to fight maladies more;
Until we set straight, our priorities,
Such maladies menace *all* countries.

Gwendolyn Rose Forrest

SEPTEMBER 6

PRIVATE DREAMS

Fore shadowing, forthcoming facts,
Do private dreams, precede our acts?
Or are they only fantasies,
That can't become realities?

Private dreams do precede our acts,
And fore shadow, forthcoming facts;
So private dreams, you alone know,
Do shape, the public life, you show.

SEPTEMBER 7

PROMISES

Promises, you have nonchalantly, not kept,
Are promises that, you have callously, swept,
Asunder, before they have germinated;
Promises, prematurely, terminated.

And promises, you've so breezily broken,
Deliver a message, that is unspoken,
But consists of these contradictory words,
"My subsequent promises should *not* be heard!"

SEPTEMBER 8

PROSPERITY

When life runs smoothly, or when it collides,
With lack, there still exists ways, to provide;
In every circumstance, swirling around,
Unseen prosperity waits, to be found.

When we believe in lack, and scarcity,
It drives us to hoard, or forever flee,
Back and forth from what, we do not desire,
While what we desire, we rarely acquire.

Shatter this shutter, shuttering the mind,
Surrounds us with prosperity, we'll find.
Yet, it's hard to define, prosperity;
It can mean this, for you, and that, for me.

But regardless of how, it is defined,
The significant thing, to keep in mind,
Is that you can produce, prosperity,
By thinking and acting, prosperously!

SEPTEMBER 9

PULLING POWER

The thoughts you think, form a magnetic field,
Pulling to you, what you intensely feel,
Starting when you, the conceiver, conceives,
Ending when you, the receiver, receives.

So pull to you, seemingly miracles,
By adhering to, these two principles:
On what you *do not want*, don't concentrate,
But on what you *do want*, elaborate!

In times of trouble, in times of sorrow,
In times when you can see, no tomorrow,
In your darkest, and most desperate hour,
Direct your thoughts! Thoughts have pulling power.

SEPTEMBER 10

PUZZLE PIECES

Life is a jigsaw puzzle, in a way,
Into which you place pieces, every day;
Assembled from aspirations, and needs,
These pieces consists of, your dreams, and deeds.

While there'll be times, puzzle pieces bedazzle,
By appearing not, to fit life's puzzle,
More often, in retrospect, you will see,
Puzzle pieces did fit in, perfectly.

SEPTEMBER 11

QUEST

If your passion's passé, and life's no fun,
Embark on a quest, with the rising sun,
The moment when upon you, it does dawn,
The time has arrived, for you, to move on.

Once you embark, upon your solo quest,
Exploring the depths, of your wilderness,
While deciding for yourself, what is best,
You will never again, settle for less.

Your quest may take you upon mountains, high,
Or deep down into desert valleys, dry,
Or meander through cities of concrete,
Or lead through their suburbs, nasty or neat.

You may quest inside isms, old, or new,
As well as inside cults, and causes, too,
Or inside, the lives of celebrities,
But you'll not find it, in any of these.

Your purpose will ever, elude you when,
You quest for it around a distant, bend;
Yet upon finding it, you must insist,
And in your quest, for it, you must persist.

Still, your purpose will continue to hide,
Until you redirect, your quest, inside;
Here, you'll find your purpose is, in the end,
To serve others, in ways, you imagine.

SEPTEMBER 12

THE QUESTION

In a wicker basket, side-by-side sat,
A teddy bear, and a calico cat;
The bear asked, "What has life in store for us?"
The cat replied, "If we knew, we might cuss."

So ask not, what life has in store, for you;
The answer could cause you, much stress, undue;
Instead, pose the question, "What must I do,
So I am of service, and happy, too?"

Then to you, let the universe express,
The ways and means, that will work for you, best;
Rather than asking, open-endedly,
You have to pose the question, properly.

SEPTEMBER 13

QUIETUDE

When in a quandary,
And quagmire of questions,
Querulously quaking,
In a quavering quest,
Quickly quiet queries,
Quelling quarrelsome qualms,
In a quintessential,
Climate called quietude.

Gwendolyn Rose Forrest

SEPTEMBER 14

RAIN

At some time in your life, love will rain,
As once more, you and your lover gain,
Pleasure from each other, while you twirl,
And thunder and lightning, rock your world.

At some time in your love, life will rain,
Causing you to cry aloud, in pain;
There will be things, you cannot go around,
But have to go through, to come out sound.

At some time in your life, past the pain,
You will understand, the role of rain;
Rain awaken, and washes away,
Negatives, you have no need to replay.

SEPTEMBER 15

RAINBOW DREAMS

Created from rain, and sunshine aglow,
The arc in the sky, known as the rainbow,
When followed, will lead to a pot, of gold;
This is in line with a legend, of old.

Today, as it did in the days, of old,
The rainbow still leads to a pot, of gold,
If in accordance with the old legend,
You follow dreams all the way to, their end.

SEPTEMBER 16

REASONS

When you are fearful and focusing down,
The darkness descends, shrouding you around;
Your faith in life falters, you feel forlorn,
And may contemplate, not meeting, the morn.

These are the dark times, when there is no light,
In a long tunnel, with no end in sight;
So in these dark times, when you see no dawn,
Summon up reasons for you to go on.

Showcasing your strengths, not your distresses,
Summon reasons from prior successes,
And hope will return to your perspective,
Leaving you no doubt that, you want to live.

Having come this far, to give up, life now,
Again you'll feel, you can make it, somehow;
Your hopelessness routed, and hope, reborn,
Give you reasons enough, to meet, the morn.

SEPTEMBER 17

RECIPE FOR RECEIVING

This is the recipe for receiving:
Give whatever you can, while believing,
Sufficiency is always, in surplus;
So scarcity can never, be robust.

Next bolster belief, with meditation,
To accelerate, the circulation,
Between that, you receive, and that, you give;
Then show your belief, by the way, you live.

Live like scarcity cannot be robust,
Because sufficiency stays in surplus;
As giving is based on, what you believe,
Voila, as you give, so do you receive.

SEPTEMBER 18

RED ROSES

Rob said he'd give Rose, red roses,
  Though when, he did not specify;
But a bouquet of red roses,
  Rose clearly saw with her mind's eye.

Expectations of, red roses,
  On her birthday, grew day, by day,
But Rose received no, red roses,
  On her birthday, to her dismay.

The next day, Rose got, red roses,
  And she no longer felt, forlorn,
For she had received, red roses,
  On her rosebush which bloomed that morn.

So expect, your expectations,
  (Including those that go amiss),
To become, manifestations,
  That may have unexpected twists.

SEPTEMBER 19

THE REFLECTION IN THE MIRROR

The reflection in the mirror,
    Currently scrutinizing me,
Over the years, has grown dearer,
    And gradually, gray like me.

The reflection, in the mirror,
    While reflecting accurately,
Cannot reflect, any clearer,
    The mystery, that makes me, me.

Gwendolyn Rose Forrest

SEPTEMBER 20

REJOICE!

A collage of color, colors the ground,
In shades of crimson, gold, copper, and brown,
Interspersed with, an occasional green;
This makes a marvelous multihued scene,
Complete, with the autumnal scrunching sound,
Of crispy, leaves underfoot, crunching down.

A collage of color, colors the lake,
With undulating leaves formed, in the wake,
Of to-be-dry-docked pontoons, and speedboats;
Soon, we'll be wearing heavy overcoats,
If unlike, flocks of fowls, we don't take flight,
To warmer climates, retaining, sunlight.

A collage of color, colors views too,
A positively, optimistic hue,
So that nothing can discolor, this day,
Transforming it into a gloomy, gray;
To delight with autumn, let us give voice;
Beauty is reason enough to, rejoice!

SEPTEMBER 21

RELATED

A tree begins life, as a seed,
With properties, it needs to lead,
Life befitting that, of a tree,
And it lives life, accordingly.

And we begin life, as we need,
With properties that help us lead,
A life befitting, a human,
And we live life, as humans can.

While each has unique properties,
We human beings, and the trees,
As members of earth's family,
We're related, intricately.

Gwendolyn Rose Forrest

SEPTEMBER 22

REMEMBRANCES

(For Tony, my son)

Resembling an airplane, awing,
A roaring, soaring, flying thing,
My son made everybody sing.

Remembrances, of a young son,
Whose joie de vivre, defused such fun,
They surface still bright, as the sun.

Remembrances, of times past known,
Perceived in the present, full blown,
They evoke a smile, or a groan.

SEPTEMBER 23

REVITALIZATION MEDITATION

I am vibrantly alive, and aglow;
Inside of me, cosmic power does flow;
My mind and my body are energized,
And my whole being is revitalized.

I see myself, as I am meant to be,
Full of vigor, vim, and vitality;
By affirming, revitalization,
I reinforce, my regeneration.

SEPTEMBER 24

RHYTHMS

Relentlessly, within the universe,
    Reoccurring rhythms play, and replay;
These rhythms aren't uniform, but diverse,
    And they manifest in, many a way.

Alternating and reciprocating,
    Unrelentingly, rhythms manifest;
Reciprocating, and alternating,
    They bring activity between, the rests.

Myriad rhythms, in the universe,
    Now are vibrating, and vacillating,
While to these rhythms, in the universe,
    Everything in it is resonating.

So find your rhythm, in the universe,
    Your unique rhythm that plays, and replays;
If in this rhythm, you remain submersed,
    You will know contentment, most of your days.

SEPTEMBER 25

RISE

Like oil must rise, to the top, of water,
Your dreams must rise, to atop, the ether,
In your realm of believability,
Before, they can become reality.

So on, the dreams that you want, do not tell,
And on the dreams that, you don't want, don't dwell,
But dwell on dreams that you want, till they rise,
Like oil, and manifest, before your eyes.

SEPTEMBER 26

RIVERS

Rivers run deep, and they run strong,
    While running their course, to the sea;
Purposefully, they flow along,
    And co-create their destiny.

Rivers rarely run, in a line;
    Rather meandering, they go,
As being flexible, they find,
    It's the best way for them, to flow.

Rivers do not run for cover,
    Whenever obstacles, abound;
Obstacles, they can't flow over,
    They find a way, to flow, around.

Rivers practice, non-resistance,
    Conforming to the curves, that be;
Rivers too, practice persistence,
    And move mountains, into the sea.

Rivers do not fret, the future,
    Nor do rivers regret, the past;
Neither tardy, nor premature,
    In the present, their lot is cast.

So try to resemble rivers,
    In your daily activity,
While purposefully, like rivers,
    You co-create your destiny.

SEPTEMBER 27

ROAD TRIP

When you reach life's high points, you want to stay,
But high points are only stops, on the way.
They're temporary stations, where you rest,
Transitory places, where you invest,
Yourself for a short, period of time,
Before resuming, life's ongoing climb.
So be humble, in the high situation,
For life is a road trip, not a staycation.

When low points are reached, you don't want to stay;
Low points, like high points, are stops, on the way,
Impermanent places, where you will find,
Negatives needing ejection, from mind,
Anchoring you down, inside small spaces,
Making you linger, in lowly, places.
So be lifted, in the low situation,
That life is a road trip, not a staycation.

SEPTEMBER 28

ROLLER COASTER RIDE

Life is a rocky roller coaster ride,
    With many ups and downs, and twists and turns;
At times, we feel we'll fall over the side,
    While our heart beats hard, and our stomach churns.

Then abruptly, we're lurched, around a bend,
    Where the going is smooth, rather than rough,
And once again, we begin to ascend;
    So we applaud ourselves, for hanging tough.

Shortly, we reach yet another, summit,
    But at this summit, while scanning, the view,
Without warning, we suddenly, plummet!
    We want to get off, but before we do,
        We think of the deadly alternative,
        Stay on the roller coaster ride, and *live!*

SEPTEMBER 29

SACRED SPOT

When we believe, it is what, it is not,
We fail to recognize, the sacred spot;
So we pilgrimage, to far-off places,
Bodies of water, and land-locked spaces,
To climates cold, to those mild, and those hot,
Any place advanced as the sacred spot.
Yet the sacred spot, which we should hold dear,
Is not in a faraway place, but near;
It is where we are, not where we are not.
Within each of us, is the sacred spot.

SEPTEMBER 30

SAY NOTHING

Circumspectly, scrutinizing them all,
The African mask, hanging on the wall,
To loose-lip figurines, with feet of clay,
Sagely says nothing that's out of the way.

So if what you'd say, would do harm, not good,
Sagely say nothing, like this mask, of wood;
The arrogant argue, talented talk,
But the sage, say nothing; they walk, the walk.

OCTOBER

OCTOBER 1

THE SCHEME OF THINGS

Do you long to live like celebrities,
Who live luxuriously, as they please?
And do you try to fill your void, with things,
Such as pricey cars, and diamond rings?

Priced moderately, costly, or cheaply,
Material things can't make you, happy;
Whether too few, too many, or enough,
All your material things are just *stuff!*

When your life runs amuck, and all's amiss,
Becoming one crisis, after crisis,
You cannot count on material things,
To see you through life's twists, turns, dips, and dings.

So discern what counts, in the scheme of things,
And appreciate the important things,
Such as, being able to lift your head,
Cleanse, clothe, feed yourself; is that enough said?

And adopt, an endowing, attitude;
Fill your void with good deeds, and gratitude.
Perversely, it's insignificant things,
We blindly covet, in the scheme of things.

OCTOBER 2

THE SEA OF POSSIBILITY

By appearing to be, risk-free,
    The shoreline of limitation,
    Lures us from our destination,
The Sea of Possibility.

It is out in the sea, we find,
    The courage and vision, we need,
    To take required risks, and succeed;
The shoreline must be left, behind.

The Sea of Possibility,
    When we show the courage to shun,
    The shoreline of limitation,
It increases our buoyancy.

OCTOBER 3

SEASONS

Now only the pine tree wears green;
　　The ash and the oak trees are bare,
While the weeping willows, when seen,
　　Display little green in their hair.

Shortly, the winter wind will blow,
　　And the flowing streamlet will freeze;
Then the spring springs, melting the snow,
　　And the trees start sprouting green leaves.

Next the summer breezes blow in,
　　Spreading the sweet scents of flowers;
After which, the fall falls again,
　　And it limits the daylight hours.

Know the seasons spin, at a pace,
　　We can neither speed up, nor slow;
So if each season, we embrace,
　　With each, we will gracefully grow.

OCTOBER 4

SECOND LOOK

Sue thought she saw a spotted snake,
Submerged in sand, beside the lake,
But no snake had her eyes been shown;
She had spotted a spotted stone.

At times, like Sue, we too receive,
Perceptions, we should not believe;
So before, swallowing the hook,
It pays to take, a second look.

OCTOBER 5

SEEDS OF TRIUMPH

Equipped with computer, calculator,
Some pens, pencils, and pieces of paper,
Tara tackled the problem, with resolve,
And ultimately, the problem, she solved.

So if by a problem, you are beset,
Do not hide your head in the sand, and fret,
As within each problem, for you to find,
Lay seeds of triumph, to plant in your mind.

OCTOBER 6

SEESAW

Opposites, such as dark and light,
    Sit on life's seesaw, together;
Consistently, like day and night,
    They seesaw, with one another.

So hang on tight, until the dawn,
    When life's downside swings, in the wind;
The seesaw of life, swinging on,
    Will show you life's upside, again.

OCTOBER 7

SEIZE THE DAY

(For Marlana, my Grandneice)

Carpe Diem means seize the day;
Believe in yourself, and the way,
To use your talents, and your skill,
Your intuition will reveal.

So act on dreams, imaginings,
For you can achieve, all the things,
Your destiny does allow.
Carpe Diem! Seize the day, now!

OCTOBER 8

SELF-FORGIVENESS

To live happily in this world, it takes,
Your self-forgiveness, for making mistakes,
As they are consequences, you have earned,
While learning life lessons, you had to learn.

So forgive yourself! Repeat if need be;
Your self-forgiveness truly sets you free.
Also, self-forgiveness enables you
To be forgiving, of another, too.

OCTOBER 9

SELF-LOVE

Have you told yourself, *I love you*, today?
If you have not, then do so, right away;
Each day if you tell yourself, *I love you,*
Your discourse and deeds will show that, you do.

As discourse and deeds are reflections of,
Fundamental feelings about self-love,
Your interactions, with everyone else,
Reflect love, or lack thereof, for yourself.

OCTOBER 10

SELF-TALK

As it's only the owner, who goes,
    On his/ her life walk, of smiles and tears,
It is only the owner, who knows,
    The self-talk, that's heard, between his/her ears.

So if the self-talk, in your thought-stream,
    Is saying, you are not good enough,
Give a big boost to your self-esteem,
    By repeating, "I have the right stuff!"

OCTOBER 11

SERENDIPITOUS GIFTS

In this imperceptibly whirling world,
Unseen, serendipitous gifts do swirl,
Minute upon minute, hour upon hour,
Like snowflakes in a swirling, snow shower.

But we're blinded by present, scenery,
Seeing what is, instead of what, could be;
The egg hides the chick, the acorn, the tree,
And some gifts hide in, serendipity.

When life proceeds, according to our plan,
We acquire its gifts, as best as we can,
But serendipitous gifts, best our best,
For these are added on top, of the rest.

Gwendolyn Rose Forrest

OCTOBER 12

SERVICE

I shall serve someone else,
Unselfishly today,
By giving of myself,
In a generous way,
For the service I give,
To someone, in some way,
Makes the life that I live,
Be purposeful each day.

OCTOBER 13

SET THE TONE

(For Vaughn, my grandson)

Begin your day, in a positive way,
And do not let negative thoughts, replay;
Instead give thanks, for your good (large and small),
Including the fact, you're alive, at all.

So make your day positive, by design;
Plant a positive mantra, in your mind.
Begin your day, in a positive way,
And set the tone, for the rest of the day.

Gwendolyn Rose Forrest

OCTOBER 14

SHARE YOUR TALENTS

Be still, let intuition intimate,
The ways and means, you're to put on your plate,
The bread you need, other things you desire,
Including the aims, to which you aspire.

So depend upon, your intuition,
To help you bring your dreams, to fruition,
And no longer will you, labor for bread;
You'll share your talents, with the world, instead.

OCTOBER 15

SHOES

Sensible women, possess no passion,
For self-torture, in the name of fashion;
Yet too many women, too often choose,
Too-high-heel shoes, over sensible shoes.

Whether one has no means or one has wealth,
These shoes present, a hazard to one's health;
Like the old Chinese, foot-binding practice,
They cripple, and cause one to walk amiss.

While too high-heel shoes are mutilating,
Insidiously, they're denigrating,
For when females are focused on their feet,
Meaningful matters go down, in defeat.

Yet little girls are brainwashed, to think of,
Hurtful shoes as sexy symbols, of love;
Girls, *but not boys,* are conditioned, to choose,
Too-high-heel shoes, over sensible shoes.

While height is gained wearing too-high-heel shoes,
Stature is lost wearing shoes that abuse;
Consequently for stature, you can't lose,
Choose to buy and to wear, sensible shoes.

OCTOBER 16

A SIBLING

(For Marie and Kay, my sisters)

A sibling is a lifetime friend,
A friend, to talk with, confide in,
A friend, to share a laugh, or two,
A friend, with whom, you can be you.

A sibling is a lifetime, friend,
A friend, to you through thick, and thin,
A friend, who loves you, right, or wrong,
A friend, whose love helps keep you, strong.

A sibling is a lifetime, friend,
A friend, through life right to the end,
And after a lifetime is through,
A sibling stays a friend. to you.

OCTOBER 17

SIGHTS AND SOUNDS

Ducks on a boat dock, soaking up some sun,
Speedboats on an across-the-river run,
And multicolored leaves, strewed on the ground,
Crackling underfoot, and rustling around.

Such are the sights and sounds, of September,
Which gradually fade, by November,
And which, on dreary days, in December,
Are the sights and sounds that, we remember.

Preserving the past, painful or pleasant,
So we can relive it, in the present,
Memories are a smoldering ember,
Igniting, the sights and sounds, we remember.

OCTOBER 18

SILENCE

Too much energy's expended,
    In excessive activity,
This, the ancients comprehended,
    And they sought silence, frequently.

But moderns are fooled by so much,
    Sensory stimuli about;
With silence, we are out of touch,
    Owing to stimuli that SHOUT!

Therefore, we would be wise, to do,
    Like those ancient women, and men,
Who entered into silence to,
    Apprehend the wisdom, therein.

Answers to many a question,
    Life unexpectedly unfolds,
Are uncovered, when we quest on,
    Inside, of silence that enfolds.

OCTOBER 19

SMILE

Contagious is a smile, or frown,
Capable of spreading around,
Respectively, a smile, or frown,
That lifts us up, or drags us down.

So when you start to come, unwound,
And turn your face, into a frown,
Just turn that frown, right upside down,
And SMILE! You'll spread a smile around.

OCTOBER 20

SNEAK PEEK

Occasionally, every mortal,
Sneaks a peek past the present's portal,
And ascertains, a preview showing,
Of the way his or her life is going.

And this sneak peek beyond the present,
Is from the universe, a present,
That resolves some of the mystery,
We have regarding, our destiny.

OCTOBER 21

SOME THINGS

Some things, no one can do for you,
For these things, only you can do;
Although these things may knock you down,
Some things, you cannot go around.

You alone, must feel your feelings,
Undergo, your body's healings,
Make up your mind, to flop, or fly,
And breathe your last breath, when you die.

Some things, you must do, on your own;
Nevertheless, you're not alone.
Come wildfire, high water, or hail,
Intuition helps you prevail.

OCTOBER 22

SPEAK ALOUD

Sometimes when afraid, speak aloud,
To remind yourself that the cloud,
Beclouding your mind, on this day,
You can disburse and blow away.

Sometimes when afraid, speak aloud,
To remind yourself that, the shroud,
Of doubt, fear, and uncertainty,
You can cast off, and act surely.

Sometimes when afraid, speak aloud,
To remind yourself, like a crowd,
Shouting, "Put your courage in gear,
And defeat, paralyzing fear."

OCTOBER 23

THE SPIDER

Seth spied the little spider,
    Running upon the wall;
A teeny-tiny spider,
    It was not large, at all.

Seth took a piece of paper,
    And rolled it 'round and 'round,
To make an insect swatter,
    And swat the spider down.

Seth swung the piece of paper;
    It made a noisy, SMACK!
But when he raised the paper,
    The spider, he'd not whacked.

Seth swung the piece of paper,
    At the spider, again,
And for the little spider,
    This time, there seemed, no win.

Nevertheless, the spider,
    Kept running very fast,
Making the blow fall wider,
    And it was safe, at last.

So like this little spider,
    To defeat, do not cede;
If to defeat, you defer,
    Defeat is guaranteed!

OCTOBER 24

SPILLS

All too frequently, we fret,
  Over the trivial things,
And too frequently, we let,
  The spills in life, clip our wings.

Misreading life's nuances,
  We make blizzards, of a breeze,
And small inconveniences,
  Of them, we make tsunamis.

While spills can cause us problems,
  And give us concern, we know,
From whence, our main problem stems,
  And it's an outsized Ego.

Most of our problems, when put,
  Into proper perspective,
They are Lilliputian, but,
  They hold large lessons to give.

So whenever you stumble,
  Experiencing a spill,
While it may make you humble,
  Your lust for life, spills can't kill.

OCTOBER 25

STAND UP

When life's events first knock you down,
    Forever, you are down, you fear,
But to staying, down on the ground,
    To this, you don't have to adhere.

Repeat "Stand Up," day and night, long,
    To help you overcome your dread,
And you'll recover, before long,
    Stand up, and with zest, move ahead.

OCTOBER 26

STATELY PALM TREES

While deciduous trees, drop their leaves,
    When daylight decreases, and cool winds come,
Stately palm trees, retaining their leaves,
    Appear unaffected, by autumn.

But appearances are deceiving,
    And fail to reflect, reality;
Stately palm trees tell autumn, from spring.
    But do so, inconspicuously.

So regarding dreams, you're pursuing,
    It's best not to boast, boisterously;
Like stately palm trees, deeds you're doing,
    Just do them, inconspicuously.

OCTOBER 27

THE STATUS QUO

Some live lives of quiet desperation,
Bouncing between, rue and resignation,
But bouncing back and forth, on the same track,
Guarantees the status quo, stays intact.

Rue and resignation, in your thought-stream,
Subsequently, drag down your self-esteem;
They make you feel, despicable and low,
But do nothing, to change, the status quo.

So do not believe you're a ne'er-do-well,
And stress your strengths; on shortcomings don't dwell.
This strengthens self-esteem, so you can go,
And do something, to change, the status quo.

When the status quo, no more satisfies,
Keeping it's tantamount to, living lies;
Choosing to change it, and going on to act,
Is how you change, the status quo, in fact.

OCTOBER 28

STEREOTYPING

Said the macaw, to the macaque, one day,
"Your tail is too short; so there is no way,
You are a monkey, for male and female,
Monkeys possess a long, prehensile tail."

Said the macaque, right back, to the macaw,
"Do not consider my short tail, a flaw.
I'm a macaque, and macaques are monkeys;
So reframe from stereotyping, please!"

Then the macaw, and the macaque, did part,
With the macaw wiser in head, and heart,
Knowing that the macaques, male and female,
Both need not have a long, prehensile tail.

Like the macaw, sometimes, in our judgment,
We are stereotypically bent;
So when we must judge, let us use ways wise.
Stereotyping ends up spreading lies.

OCTOBER 29

STILL YOURS

No relative, colleague, friend, or lover,
Can create happiness, for another,
As happiness originates within;
So prime your pump of happiness often.

Prime it more often, if you're under stress,
Due to physical or mental illness;
In your happiness, you retain a voice,
And your happiness is still yours, by choice.

OCTOBER 30

STREET SENSE

Crowded city streets convey,
A sense of haste, at midday,
When workers scurry around,
Crowded city streets, downtown.

Tree-lined city streets evoke,
A sense of peaceable poke,
When suppertime rolls around,
And neighborhoods quiet down.

Sporting city streets ferry,
A bold sense of revelry,
When sometime, around midnight,
Revelers voice their delight.

Empty city streets carry,
A sense of expectancy,
When dawn spawns, an empty day,
To fill, however, we may.

OCTOBER 31

STRESS, CHANGE, AND UNCERTAINTY

To cope with stress, change, and uncertainty,
In the fast paced, space-age society,
Stop seeking, without; start seeking, within;
Alone in silence is how, to begin.

When outside intervention is needed,
Silence helps you, to find it, and heed it;
Seek first, in silence, and successfully,
You'll cope with stress, change, and uncertainty.

NOVEMBER

NOVEMBER 1

SUDDEN STORM

Suddenly, growing gusts of wind,
Begin buffeting tree leaves; then,
Striking streaking strips, of splendor,
Precede rolling roars, of thunder.

Raindrops splatter down, through tree leaves,
As treetops bend down, with much ease;
A terrifying, sudden storm,
From out of the blue, starts to form.

Sometimes life is stormy, like this,
When suddenly, things go amiss;
Then, as suddenly, the storm's gone.
Although things have changed, life goes on.

Once again, the sun is shining,
And life shows, its silver lining;
So when a sudden storm, takes form,
Your task is to weather, the storm.

Gwendolyn Rose Forrest

NOVEMBER 2

SUNFLOWERS AND DAISIES

Sunflowers and daisies, in the backyard,
Make crying the blues, not easy, but hard,
For they're flexible, yet firm, and yellow,
And they never forget, to wave hello.

Standing their ground, with their hands, on their hips,
They fail to fall apart, when the wind whips;
So when winds of woe, start to whip, at you,
Do as the sunflowers and daisies, do.

Sunflowers and daisies upon, the wall,
Brighten up the romper room, down the hall;
With their funny faces, and yellow hue,
They easily brighten perspectives, too.

Primarily, it's perspective on life,
That causes us such sadness, stress, and strife.
Ordinary things are what make life, bright;
All we must do is to look at them right.

NOVEMBER 3

SUNRISE

Seeing the sun rise over the city,
    It is a breathtaking sight, to behold;
Between tall buildings, lofty and pretty,
    Gradually grows a bright ball, of gold.

And seeing the sun rise behind your eyes,
    This also is breathtaking, to behold;
From out of amorphous mist does arise,
    An idea that's more precious, than gold.

NOVEMBER 4

SUNSET AND AUTUMN

Shades of purple, pink, orange, and yellow,
Merging with shades, of blue and black shadow,
Congregate along, time's continuum,
And make an awesome, sunset and autumn.

Sunset and autumn, like sunrise and spring,
They are pregnant, with potential, to bring,
You limitation, or liberation,
That's in line with, your imagination.

Likewise, your sunset and autumn will bring,
A phase in your life fit for, flowering,
But you must choose, to be, adventuresome,
To make your sunset and autumn, *awesome!*

NOVEMBER 5

SUNSHINE

To clear away the clutter,
    That is cluttering, your mind,
Just open your mind's shutter,
    And let sunshine in, to find...

Those dark and shady places,
    Wherein double doubt does howl,
Around the sunken spaces,
    Where, primordial fears prowl.

Exposed, they lose their bluster;
    Doubt and fear become benign.
So when freed, from this clutter,
    Sunshine enlightens your mind.

Gwendolyn Rose Forrest

NOVEMBER 6

A SYNCHONOUS EVENT

The sun's descent, within the western sky,
It's a challenge, to the uncovered eye,
But the moon's ascent, in the eastern sky,
It's easy on the eye, while moving high.

Both bodies are beautiful, full and bright,
One sending, the other receiving light;
Together, they make a stupendous sight,
As descending day, meets ascending night.

To be present, in this place, at this time,
For no other purpose, reason, or rhyme,
Than to see the sun set, and the moon climb,
It is an honor that is so, sublime.

Most times, we're too preoccupied, to see,
The breathtaking phenomenal, beauty,
Occurring in a synchronous event,
That comes at an unexpected moment.

NOVEMBER 7

TAKING CARE OF BUSINESS

To keep it running smoothly, without snare,
The business of your life needs constant care;
So taking care of business, properly,
It's a fulltime responsibility.

This leaves you no time, in which to bother,
Taking care of business, for another;
Ownership of the business must be shown.
The business you take care of is your own.

Gwendolyn Rose Forrest

NOVEMBER 8

TALENT

Talent, defined, is the ability,
To do a certain thing, successfully;
However, success is not guaranteed.
Talent must be put to use, to succeed.

When service is talent's primary goal,
The result from using it is two-fold,
For talent used, to perform a good act,
Also keeps our integrity, intact.

NOVEMBER 9

TERROR

When some have no law, on which they can stand,
Terror's the *de facto* law, in the land;
Those living in terror, day after day,
Know it in a very, visceral way.

Recognizing they have no law, to wield,
They tiptoe through society's minefield,
Repressing rage that makes the stomach burn,
While meeting with terror, at every turn.

Terror is a symbol that's understood,
Little old lady, entire neighborhood,
Employer, grocer, judge, juror, police;
Terror is drones dropping bombs that don't cease.

Ultimately, the terrorized will rise,
Employing tactics used for their demise,
Or against terror, they will take a stand,
And not let terror, *in fact*, rule the land.

Gwendolyn Rose Forrest

NOVEMBER 10

THE THINGS IN WHICH YOU HAVE NO VOICE

You may not choose, who makes you cry,
But you can choose, whom to forgive;
You may not choose, the way, you die,
But you can choose, the way, you live.

The things, in which, you have no voice,
You still can choose to win, or lose,
About these things, you have a choice.
How you respond; this, you can choose.

NOVEMBER 11

THINGS THAT ARE MINE

The things that are mine, rightfully,
They're my responsibility;
The other things, accordingly,
They're outside, my authority.

So discerning, the difference,
Not only makes good common sense,
But is of utmost, importance,
Since, I live with the consequence.

And while our destinies entwine,
Your destiny's yours, mine is mine;
Together, some things, we can bear,
But other things, we cannot share.

The things that are yours, you pursue;
The things that are mine, I must do,
For self-responsibility,
It frees me from dependency.

NOVEMBER 12

THOUGHTS

Flitting around on unseen wings,
Thoughts are doubly, creative things;
Internally, what they create,
Externally, they duplicate.

And in accord with, altitude,
Thoughts also affect, attitude;
As lofty thoughts, keep thoughts, aloft,
Upon lowly thoughts, keep thoughts off.

NOVEMBER 13

TIES

The invisible ties that bind,
They're ties mesmerizing, the mind,
Ties binding, irrevocably,
Ties from which, we'll never be free.

The invisible ties that bind,
They are the equalizing kind,
Of birth, breath, and mortality,
And these ties make us family.

The invisible ties that bind,
They're ties, the cosmos does assign,
Ties that make us, what we will be,
And tie us to our destiny.

Gwendolyn Rose Forrest

NOVEMBER 14

TILTED

Failure is not exactly, what it seems,
　　As it is feedback, for we do not know,
All of the avenues, ways, and/or means,
　　The universe directs us, to follow.

We learn the what, when, where, why, and the how,
　　From feedback that's reaped from, what we did sow.
Till then, that we sowed is enough, for now;
　　So we can expect success, tomorrow.

As the universe tilts toward success,
　　We are tilted, in the very same way;
Therefore, what we sow, tends to manifest,
　　And success tilts toward us, every day.

NOVEMBER 15

TIME ALLOTMENT

The time allotment, allotted you,
 Was allotted you, before your birth,
And there is not one thing, you can do,
 That extends your time, upon the earth.

As each yesterday, or tomorrow,
 Either is a dream, or memory,
You've no more time, from which, to borrow;
 Your time allotment's *today*, only.

NOVEMBER 16

TIME ALONE

There comes a time, in each day,
When you need some time, away,
From the internet highway,
And those at work, or at play.

Time away from radio,
Television, stereo,
Family, friends, mobile phone,
You need time to spend, alone.

Time alone is a mainstay,
Anchor, lest you drift away,
In the din and confusion,
Of another's illusion.

So at some point, in each day,
See to it, you slip away,
Into silence that, you own;
Spend some quiet time, alone.

NOVEMBER 17

TIME TO BEGIN AGAIN

If passion has ebbed, to an end,
And life is no fun, you are in,
A situation that's grown thin,
And it's time to begin, again.

Times past of sunshine, or of rain,
Forever, in the past remain;
So don't let times past detain when,
It is time to begin, again.

Like the serpent changes, its skin,
In season, and without chagrin,
You too must change, and you'll know when,
It is time to begin, again.

While change may cause some stress, and strain,
As well as cause pleasure, or pain,
Life dictates that change shall reign when,
It is time to begin, again.

NOVEMBER 18

TIMING

Softly falling snow, silences the sound,
    Of vehicles on busy streets below,
But daunting questions in mind that resound,
    Aren't silenced by, the softly falling snow:

"How did I get to the place, I now sit?
    Was it by accident, or by design?
If by accident, is that all to it?
    Or if by design, is the design, mine?"

"Are my dreams and deeds, all, I require,
    To climb the crags, I've chosen, for climbing?
Or do the outcomes, to which, I aspire,
    In addition, depend upon, timing?"

Timing is not, the workings, of the mind,
    For it is the cosmic rhythm and rhyme,
Of other factors that are intertwined,
    With dreams and deeds, taking place, at the time.

So outcomes do dependent, upon timing,
    (Foreseen and unforeseen factors, we'll know),
And while life's a cloudy crag, we're climbing,
    It is awesome, like softly falling snow.

NOVEMBER 19

TIPPING POINT

Akin to the way, you are, what you think,
You are and display, what you eat, and drink.
The tipping point is reached, when sweets, and such,
Go over the top, and become, too much.

By keeping yourself, hail, hardy, and fit,
The tipping point, you can circumvent it;
So to stay healthy, in body, and mind,
Maintain balance, when you think, drink, or dine.

Gwendolyn Rose Forrest

NOVEMBER 20

TO BE TRANSFORMED

Just like the seed must die, to be,
Transformed into, the living tree,
The same holds true, for you, and me,
To be transformed, die too, must we.

Holding pleasure, but also pain,
To be transformed is balm, and bane;
Unexpected, or expected,
Distinct phases are detected:

Termination, separation,
Dislocation, devastation,
Rebirth, reconciliation,
Concord, and continuation.

Examples of transformation,
Include birth, and maturation,
Marriage, divorce, and retirement;
Part of us dies, with each event.

So we die, continually,
And at the same time, live to see,
We are altered, internally,
And we're altered, externally.

To be transformed means to shed tears,
To tread the unknown, and face fears,
To die, and to be born, again;
To be transformed means to, begin.

NOVEMBER 21

TOADSTOOLS

When Wong went to bed, last night,
There was not a one, in sight,
But at dawn, he looked around,
And toadstools dotted the ground.

From nowhere it seemed, they came,
With a short stay as their aim,
For as fast as, they'd appeared,
Overnight, they disappeared.

Sometimes, troubles are toadstools,
Behaving by unknown rules;
By appearing overnight,
They make us frantic, with fright.

Sometimes, these toadstools too,
Overnight, vanish from view;
So if we endure, till dawn,
We could find these toadstools, gone.

Gwendolyn Rose Forrest

NOVEMBER 22

TODAY

Yesterday is in the past, to stay,
And it can't be changed, in anyway,
While tomorrow's always, on its way,
But never comes; it becomes today.

With no tomorrow, or yesterday,
In which to have an actual stay,
To do whatever we will, or may,
The only time we have is *today.*

NOVEMBER 23

TOO MANY WARS

Too many wars, we have waged,
    When engorged egos did collide;
Too many wars, we have waged,
    Because too many, leaders lied.

Too many wars, we have waged,
    For profit, property, and pride;
Too many wars, we have waged,
    With righteousness claimed, by each side.

Too many wars, we have waged,
    With the ways of war, glorified;
Too many wars, we have waged.
    Too many innocents have died.

Too many wars, we have waged,
    Denying war is genocide;
Too many wars, we have waged,
    To keep peace, but keep war in stride.

Gwendolyn Rose Forrest

NOVEMBER 24

TREASURE

(For Sherlane, my friend since age sixteen)

An ice skating rink, in the sun,
Entices us to come have fun,
But an unlit rink, in the dark,
It is not enticing, but stark.

However, when bathed in moonlight,
The rink is enticing, at night;
An ice skating rink, we can say,
It is a treasure, night and day.

Likewise, friendship is a treasure,
Treasure, too precious, to measure;
When life is as bright as, the sun,
Friendship intensifies the fun.

And when life is unlit, and stark,
Friendship illuminates the dark;
So friendship, like a lasting link,
It's a treasure that does not shrink.

NOVEMBER 25

THE TREE OF KNOWLEDGE

The tree of knowledge is a tree of light;
Eating its fruit illumines the mind's night,
But also opens a Pandora's Box.
The tree of knowledge is a paradox.

The tree of knowledge bears both good and bad,
Making us happy, or making us sad;
The fruit we consume, and the quantity,
Together determine life's quality.

The tree of knowledge provides us a voice,
Against superstition, and gives us choice;
So the tree of knowledge helps us, to live,
With more freedom, and we have more, to give.

Gwendolyn Rose Forrest

NOVEMBER 26

TRUST YOURSELF!

Trust yourself! By past deeds, you are not bound,
Nor can others' opinions, hold you down.

Trust yourself! To your highest self, be true;
You have a competent compass, in you.

Trust yourself! You'll find self-trust does bring,
Freedom to be yourself, and *do your thing!*

NOVEMBER 27

TWILIGHT

Eastward, gathering darkness quickly grows,
While westward, waning sunlight softly glows,
And for a while, before the fall, of night,
The sky's aglow, with the glow of, twilight.

The incandescent atmosphere, above,
Brings to mind, the olive branch, and the dove,
And for a while, before the fall, of night,
The world appears warfare-free, at twilight.

When enough of us, start practicing peace,
War upon war on the planet, will cease;
So for a while, during the day, or night,
Practice the peace that's perceived, at twilight.

Gwendolyn Rose Forrest

NOVEMBER 28

TWIST AND TURN

Butterfly fish swim through the reef, in pairs,
Twisting and turning, seemingly, sans cares,
But things are not always, as one would wish,
Even for beautiful, butterfly fish.

Twisting and turning is the way, life goes,
On a course that in advance, no one knows;
So like butterfly fish, adapt a bit,
And be able to twist and turn, with it.

NOVEMBER 29

TWO WORLDS

Two worlds exist simultaneously:
One world, we can hear, taste, touch, smell, and see,
While the other world is the world, we think,
And these two worlds are not always, in synch.

Nonetheless both, simultaneously,
Create and sustain, our reality;
Therefore, our well-being depends, upon,
Balance, in two worlds, and between, each one.

NOVEMBER 30

UNCONDITIONAL LOVE

For love to be unconditional love,
    It must be given absolutely free,
And we are capable of giving love,
    That is given, unconditionally.

Unconditional love's not, self-serving,
    For it is an unselfish act, unmatched;
Recipients need not be, deserving,
    For it is given, with no strings, attached.

Unconditional love, allows us to,
    Use our compassionate ability,
To love ourselves, others, and things, and to,
    Love the beloved, unconditionally.

Unconditional love is unswerving,
    As it is an irrevocable act;
Only the highest is this love serving.
    Unconditional love remains, intact.

DECEMBER

DECEMBER 1

UNFOLDING MYSTERIES

As life is an unfolding mystery,
Offering untold possibility,
Outside of the farthest flashing quasars,
There exist yet-to-be-discovered stars.

And inside, the minute organism,
More minute ones wait, for us to find them.
As life is unfolding to what comes next,
We can't comprehend its complete context.

Yet periodically, we awake,
To new possibilities that will take,
Us far beyond present, profundities,
For, we too are unfolding mysteries.

DECEMBER 2

UNIFIED

Deliberate please, upon dancing leaves,
Steadily shimmying, in a brisk breeze;
Suspend for a while, your turbulent thoughts,
The why mes, if onlys, ought nots, and oughts.

When your thoughts have been displaced, and dispersed,
You'll be unified with the universe;
And when totally absorbed, and entranced,
You will perceive enlightenment, perchance.

DECEMBER 3

UNINTENDED CONSEQUENCES

Some bits of bread drop, while we dined,
    Specks of sand, shoes swipe, from the bay,
Or random thoughts, come into mind,
    And they completely change, the day.

Unintended consequences,
    Can cause us to chuckle, or cry,
But most times, the evidence is,
    So subtle, it passes us by.

DECEMBER 4

UNION

While he was of non-noble ancestry,
She was a princess, a pure pedigree,
And nimble of foot, where he'd likely fall.
She was almost as short, as he was tall.

While he cooked most everything, by the book,
She ate most anything, but could not cook.
She, a princess, and he, plain people's son,
They appeared to have little, in common.

Thus their union seemed, unlikely to last,
And quickly become, a fling of the past,
But for Princess, the dog, and master, man,
Although it seemed doomed, their union did stand.

In a union, eons fashioned, and tried,
With other animals, humans are tied;
So when other animals are at risk,
We are, in the final, analysis.

DECEMBER 5

THE UNIVERSAL URGE TO CREATE

It's the universal urge to create,
That is the impetus, to procreate,
Make religion, science, technology,
And music, art, dance, plays, and poetry,

It's the universal urge to create,
That is the impetus making us make,
Order from chaos continually,
And perpetuate possibility.

DECEMBER 6

UP AND DOWN THE STAIRCASE

Empowered by the cosmos, we ascend,
Up the staircase, and into life begin,
Turning dreams into deeds, along our way.
We go up the staircase, until one day . . .

It's down the staircase, imperceptibly,
We go, at first, later noticeably;
Deeds we performed, in the past easily,
Now we perform them, with difficulty.

Going up, we are unaware of time;
Going down, we are aware of decline.
At death, our power is recycled; then,
Up the staircase power goes once again.

DECEMBER 7

VALIDATION

Do not look outward, to somebody else,
To provide validation, for yourself;
If you adopt another's illusion,
You stay in a state of, vast confusion.

Validation, from outside, your purview,
It is invalid, when applied, to you,
Owing to this unassailable, fact:
Self-validation is an *inside* act.

DECEMBER 8

THE VEIL

Starting from the time, of our birth,
  Until the time, of our demise,
(Meaning every day, we're on earth),
  The veil is covering, our eyes.

Composed of culture, the veil, to wit,
  Is unavoidably acquired,
And all things are filtered, through it,
  Including, what's shunned, or desired.

Knowing the veil covers our eyes,
  Helps us judge, more impartially,
In a manner, which otherwise,
  Would not be, in the least, veil-free.

DECEMBER 9

VICE, VIOLENCE, AND VALUE

Too many criminals, too few police,
In the neighborhoods preserving the peace;
Too many folks, for vice, and violence,
Too few are for reason, and common sense.

Too many, for greed, and retribution,
Too few, with values for reformation;
Too many prisons, too few policies,
That value people, in the remedies.

Reoccurring vice and violence send,
A message saying, we need to expend,
Time revising, the current remedies,
And replace them with people policies.

Gwendolyn Rose Forrest

DECEMBER 10

VIEWS

Dillydally in the valley,
    And this behavior limits you;
Rise above the narrow valley,
    And you'll gain a mountaintop view.

From above, you'll see solutions,
    That from below, you could not do,
And you'll fashion resolutions,
    Weighing, a mountaintop view, too.

DECEMBER 11

VISION

Our inner vision, not our eyes,
    Sees with unerring clarity,
And what we need to recognize,
    Inner vision reveals, clearly.

When we look through physical eyes,
    We see present realities;
With inner vision, we cognize,
    And see new possibilities.

So where a closed door stood before,
    Inner vision, interceded,
We envision an open door,
    And our progress, unimpeded.

DECEMBER 12

WATER FOR ELEPHANTS

A mother elephant, and her baby,
Do not worry where the water will be,
When from a waterhole, somewhere around,
They again need water, around sundown.

They know worry is wasted energy,
With no effect on, what is, or will be;
So like elephants, eliminate stress.
And do not worry, but expect success.

DECEMBER 13

WATERFALLS

Beginning as trickles, in a mountain massif,
    They gather momentum, in their downward free fall,
Until they cascade over a steep precipice,
    No longer as trickles; now they're a waterfall.

Incipient ideas, start as trickles, too,
    And gather momentum, from thoughts of, "I can do,"
Until they cascade, over skepticism to,
    Become a waterfall that, anyone can view.

So water your trickles, with facts, faith, and silence,
    To fortify them, in order that they don't stall,
At detractor's doubt, disdain, and indifference,
    Until they become a viable waterfall.

DECEMBER 14

WAVES AND WOES

Wild waves forcefully fling,
    Themselves, upon the beach,
Engulfing everything,
    That's in their roiling reach.

Chaotic confusion,
    Is how these waves appear,
But of this conclusion,
    It is best, to steer clear.

With their perturbation
    Wrecking heck and havoc,
Undue undulation,
    These roiling waves are NOT.

So, if you can see waves,
    Shaping stones into sand,
You can see, woes are waves,
    Shaping you, like a hand.

DECEMBER 15

WEBS

Spider webs ensnare, the unwary,
    By appearing fragile, and benign,
And they ensnare, insidiously,
    For these webs emit, no warning sign.

Lies are webs that insidiously,
    Appear to be clever and benign,
But one leads to others, until we,
    Become inextricably, entwined.

DECEMBER 16

WHAT WILL YOU BE ABLE TO SAY?

Near the end of your life journey,
    What will you be able to say?
You amassed a lot, of money,
    But you frittered a lot, away?

Or will you be able to say,
    You are proud of the life you led,
For in a significant way,
    Other people's lives, your life fed?

DECEMBER 17

THE WHEEL OF LIFE

Fresh salmon fry swim downstream, to the sea,
Where they play, eat, or are eaten, quickly;
Years later survivors, no longer fry,
Struggle back upstream, where they spawn, then die.

First, like fresh fry, we are the young, at play,
While the ancestors, and elders are they;
Then, we are the elders, who will one day,
Be ancestors, of the young yet, to play.

The wheel of life continues, revolving,
While all things within it, keep evolving,
Now manifesting, and then dissolving,
But life's mystery, we're never solving.

DECEMBER 18

WHEN

From schoolhouses across America,
To those on Continental Africa,
Resources are siphoned off, for the aim,
Of waging war, and they're never, regained.

As violence, begets more violence,
Violence is clearly, the consequence,
Passed on to seceding, generations,
And they commit more abominations.

When, will the sitting administrations,
With social-economic, frustrations,
Faced by most administrations, before,
Forbear from waging any form, of war?

When enough of us cede, in each nation,
Competition, for cooperation,
We'll insist that all humanity,
Live without war, and with dignity.

DECEMBER 19

WHEN THE WORLD OUTSIDE BECOMES TOO HEAVY

When the world outside, becomes too heavy,
　　Take a break from this world of clashing wills,
Clanging symbols, hidden hypocrisy,
　　Mundane mediocrity, and like ills.

When the world outside, becomes too heavy,
　　Retreat in silence, to the world inside;
Here, be renewed, and you'll soon be ready,
　　To return to the world that waits, outside.

Gwendolyn Rose Forrest

DECEMBER 20

WHEN YOU CANNOT SAVE THE WORLD

When you cannot save the world,
Help a boy, or help a girl,
Or a woman, or a man;
Just help, any way, you can.

When you cannot save the world,
Help an elm, or a squirrel,
With your wallet, or your hand;
Just help, any way, you can.

When you cannot save the world,
Or make peace in it, unfurl,
Address an atrocity;
Help someone or thing, to be.

When you cannot save the world,
Help you give is like a pearl.
When you give help from your heart,
It's enough; you've done your part.

DECEMBER 21

WINGS

The woeful wooly worm slithered, slowly,
Feeling forlorn, without worth, and lowly,
When she came upon, a lovely creature,
And beautiful wings were its best, feature.

The woeful wooly worm asked, breathlessly,
"Where can I buy some wings like yours, for me?"
The creature replied, "Wings, you cannot buy;
You must go within, if you want to fly."

The woeful wooly worm, spun a cocoon,
Went within it, and on emerging, soon,
Discovered a fact that lifted her high;
She had grown wings, and was a butterfly.

Like the woeful wooly worm, you can be,
Feeling forlorn, without worth, and lowly,
Trying to buy joy, prove your worth with things,
Or you can go within you, and grow wings.

Gwendolyn Rose Forrest

DECEMBER 22

WINTER BLASTS

Another winter blast, before the spring,
Hits hard and fast, transforming everything;
Now tree branches gleam, like crystallized glass,
And brittle has become, the gleaming grass.

O how, the howling wind does shift, and blow,
Creating shifting patterns, in the snow,
Skimming the surface, of the frozen lake,
That holds no skaters daft enough, to skate.

At time, adversities are winter blasts,
That hit us hard and fast, before they pass;
So when we're hit by winter blasts, like these,
Our task is to outlast, adversities.

DECEMBER 23

WINTER NIGHT IMAGERY

On a star-studded, winter night,
When the sky's borealis, bright,
Sculpturing snow, skillfully shapes,
Images of white wedding cakes,
Artic foxes, big polar bears,
And little seal pups with small ears.

On a star-studded, winter night,
When the sky's borealis, bright,
And enough of us, imagine,
That *all* men, women, and children,
Are intrinsically, of worth,
We will bring about peace, on earth.

Gwendolyn Rose Forrest

DECEMBER 24

WITH WORDS

She creates, eye-catching pictures,
    By initially selecting,
Vivid colors, for her mixtures;
    Then accepting, or rejecting,
        Colors, till they sing, like sun-up songbirds,
        She creates, eye-catching pictures, with words.

She invents, enticing incense,
    By initially selecting,
Ingredients for, their sweet scents;
    Then accepting, or rejecting,
        Sweet scents, till they sing, like sun-up songbirds,
        She invents, enticing incense, with words.

She prepares, flavorful, fine food,
    By initially selecting,
Flavors, which are tongue-tasting good;
    Then accepting, or rejecting,
        Flavors, till they sing, like sun-up songbirds,
        She prepares, flavorful, fine food, with words.

She fashions, fabulous fashions,
    By initially selecting,
Fabrics eliciting passions;
    Then accepting, or rejecting,
        Fabrics, till they sing, like sun-up songbirds,
        She fashions, fabulous fashions, with words.

She creates, aural artistry,
    By initially selecting,
Thoughts woven, in her tapestry;
        Then accepting, or rejecting,
            Her thoughts, till they sing, like sun-up songbirds,
            She creates, aural artistry, with words.

And creativity is meant,
    To be expressed, in an action;
So when we allow it to vent,
        It gives us, great satisfaction,
            That stirs us to sing, like sun-up songbirds,
            And to be heard, like she is heard, with words.

Gwendolyn Rose Forrest

DECEMBER 25

WITHOUT CHATTER

Silently, soft snowflakes,
    Unlike chattering sleet,
Change lackluster landscapes,
    Without making a peep.

So to change, your dreamscapes,
    From theory, into fact,
Be like silent snowflakes,
    And without chatter, *act!*

DECEMBER 26

WORDS

As words are self-creating tools,
    Be mindful of how you use, them;
Since they work for sages, and fools,
    It is easy to misuse, them.

So choose your words, to spread a smile,
    To other people's minds, and hearts,
And when you write, write words worthwhile,
    For words create their counterparts.

DECEMBER 27

WORK

Work is not linked, to pleasure, like leisure,
    But work and leisure, are not opposite,
For work, like leisure, can produce pleasure;
    This makes work and leisure, side-by-side sit.

Work's reward, is partly in the doing,
    Regardless of the type of work, you do;
When from your work, pleasure is ensuing,
    Work's not work, but self-expression, for you.

DECEMBER 28

THE WORLD THAT IS AND AS IT COULD BE

Of the eight planets, encircling the sun,
To date, Planet Earth is the only one,
Upon which humans make a world, of it,
And this world is made, mostly, by habit.

Habit includes deeds debasing females,
And warfare, from which, the world that is ails.
And atrocities, sold as tradition,
They're blindly pursued, with repetition.

So humans spinning, imperceptibly,
While acting along, or collectively,
Purposefully, and/or haphazardly,
Make the world that is, continuously.

Each and every human has, in effect,
On the world that is, some kind of effect;
While living his or her life, day by day,
Each one molds the world that is, in some way,

So it's no wonder, the world that is grows,
In myriad directions as it goes,
Unfolding like lotus blossoms, unfold,
And it conforms, not to any one mold.

The world that is, and not, as it could be,
Too often erupts in, hostility,
When frictional factions, all in a whirl,
Make war in this rapidly shrinking, world.

Gwendolyn Rose Forrest

War wastes people, along with, the planet.
What is it regarding war, we don't get?
If lessons, from previous wars, aren't learned,
Both, the people and the planet, will burn.

Cultural clashes and adverse actions,
Resulting in ruthless, interactions,
These must be banned, in perpetuity,
To make the world that is, as it could be.

DECEMBER 29

THE YEARS

(Remembering Shirley Rae, my friend from first grade)

The laughter, and the tears,
What happened, to the years?
A diaphanous dream,
The years gone by now seem.

The closer that death nears,
The faster flee, the years:
This causes me to cry,
"My how, the years do fly!"

And years, gone by, endear,
Not one, but every year,
To live my destiny,
That does remain, for me.

So live your coming years,
With fewer tears, and fears;
When all is said, and done,
Too soon, the years are gone.

Gwendolyn Rose Forrest

DECEMBER 30

YOUR BOOK OF LIFE

Your book of life is written, in a way,
That you write, a part of it, everyday,
Each day delivers to you, a blank page,
On which, to write something silly, or sage.

And the deeds that you do, both large and small,
Deliver your book's message, overall.
You write your book of life with wrong, and right;
So you would be wise, to watch what, you write.

DECEMBER 31

ZERO HOUR

Zero hour is both, nadir and zenith,
And the hour, of much, mystery and myth,
The hour, beginning, and ending, each day,
The hour, tomorrow, turns into, today.

We spend our lives, through sunshine, and shower,
Zigzagging our way, to the zero hour,
But when it is reached, instead of the end,
Zero hour's the hour, to begin again.

ABOUT THE AUTHOR

G WENDOLYN ROSE FORREST was born and reared in Detroit, Michigan. Writing has always been an integral part of her life. She is a former social worker, civil/human rights advocate, and employment/training coordinator. As the Director of Research for the State of Michigan's, Wayne County Charter Commission, she helped write the county's first home-rule charter. She also served as an economic-opportunity administrator in Georgia. As a Certified Fund Raising Executive, she assisted colleges and universities in Michigan, Oregon, and Illinois to achieve their financial goals. She holds a Bachelor's Degree in sociology, a Master's Degree in public administration, and currently resides in the Detroit Metropolitan Area.

Review Requested:
If you loved this book, would you please provide a review at Amazon.com?

CPSIA information can be obtained at www.ICGtesting.com
Printed in the USA
BVOW02s2143270915

419784BV00001B/1/P